Landscapes of Learning

Lifelong learning in rural communities

Edited by Fred Gray

OXFORD BROOKES
UNIVERSITY
LIBRARY

HARCOURT HILL
01865 488222

D0260379

Published by the National Institute of Adult Continuing Education
(England and Wales)
21 De Montfort Street
Leicester
LE1 7GE

Company registration no. 2603322
Charity registration no. 1002775

First published 2002

Editorial © Fred Gray, 2002
Individual chapters © individual contributors, 2002

ACC. NO.		FUND
78226409		EDUG
LOC.	CATEGORY	PRICE
ET	STAN	15-95

– 3 MAR 2006

CLASS No.
374.941 LAN

OXFORD BROOKES
UNIVERSITY LIBRARY

All rights reserved. No reproduction, copy or transmission of this publication
may be made without the written permission of the publishers, save in
accordance with the provisions of the Copyright, Designs and Patents Act
1988, or under the terms of any license permitting copying issue by the
Copyright Licensing Agency.

promoting adult learning

NIACE, the National Institute of Continuing Adult Education, has a broad
remit to promote lifelong opportunities for adults. NIACE works to develop
increased participation in education and training. It aims to do this for those
who do not have easy access because of class, gender, age, race, language and
culture, learning difficulties or disabilities, or insufficient financial resources.

You can find NIACE online at www.niace.org.uk

Cataloguing in Publication Data
A CIP record of this title is available from the British Library

ISBN   1 86201 093 5

Design and layout by
Publish2day Oxford Limited, Oxfordshire

Printed and bound in the UK by
Alden Press, Oxford

Contents

Contributors

Veronica Adamson and *Jane Plenderleith* both left the services of the University of the Highlands and Islands during 2000. In June of that year they established Glenaffric Ltd., a professional development consultancy that aims to take a sensible, measured approach to the use of new technologies in education and management development.

Marie Askham has followed personal and professional interests in lifelong learning for many years. She has worked as an Open University humanities tutor for over a decade and became a part-time tutor for the University of Cambridge Board of Continuing Education in the early 1990s. She is currently working on a PhD on anti-militarism in British women's writing between the wars.

Roseanne Benn has worked in adult education for more years than she likes to remember, first at Hillcroft College, Surbiton, then at the Department of Lifelong Learning at Exeter University. Her 15 years at Exeter have made her very conscious of the particular issues facing both learners and the providers of learning opportunities in rural areas. She is currently working on both distance learning and widening participation initiatives, with rurality an important dimension in both.

Ian Davidson joined the Department of Lifelong Learning at the University of Wales, Bangor in 1995, following teaching and managerial work in credit and Access. In his current role he teaches and co-ordinates courses in writing, literature and fine art and has a keen interest in research and use of new technologies.

Len Graham has 30 years' experience of higher and continuing education, lecturing in drama and youth and community education. He project-managed Rural Broadnet for Wolverhampton University for five years. Currently he manages CEKnowledgeNorthWest.com, knowledge brokerage for North West Universities Association. He has chaired committees for the Arts Council and Gulbenkian Foundation.

Fred Gray is Professor of Continuing Education at the University of Sussex and for over a decade was the Director of the University's Centre for Continuing Education. He was a founding member of the Rural Network of the Universities Association for Continuing Education.

William R. Jones has worked in university adult education throughout his career, beginning at the University of Southampton. Since 1998 he has been Professor of Lifelong Learning at the University of Newcastle upon Tyne, and Director of the University's Centre for Lifelong Learning, which provides adult learning over the large and mainly rural region of Northumberland and Cumbria. His research interests are in the history and practice of adult education and in his original discipline of English literature and, especially, regional, rural and maritime writing.

John R. Nicholson co-ordinates widening participation initiatives based in the University of East Anglia's Centre for Continuing Education. He is committed to promoting the public understanding of science, having organised science festivals and given lectures and workshops in the UK, Australia and New Zealand. He has contributed to research and curriculum development in Africa and written science books for use in primary and secondary schools.

Sue Pester is the Lifelong Learning Officer at the University of Wales, Aberystwyth. Dr. Pester is responsible for several widening access schemes and manages the community-based, Adult Guidance Project. She is also the Convenor of the Rural Network of the Universities Association for Continuing Education.

John O'Donoghue's wide range of educational experience includes working as a school teacher and LEA officer. He is Deputy Director and Head of Pedagogic Research at the Delta Institute, Wolverhampton University, and specialises in the use of technology in educational applications. In 1998 he joined an UNESCO-funded group researching educational technology and was appointed Visiting Research Fellow, University of Wollongong, Australia.

Susan Oosthuizen was brought up in South Africa, from which stems her keen interest in widened participation. She is Staff Tutor in Landscape History at the University of Cambridge Board of Continuing Education and manages widened participation projects in the Fenland on behalf of the Board.

Peter Ryley is Academic Co-ordinator in Lifelong Learning in the Centre for Lifelong Learning at the University of Hull. He has worked in rural outreach education for High Peak College in Derbyshire and the University of Hull. He is currently researching the historical origins of contemporary Green Politics.

Part 1

1

Introduction: learning and the countryside

Fred Gray

Introduction

The starting point of this book is that lifelong learning in rural communities is a neglected but important subject. Neglected in that, during recent decades, both government in its various guises and the educational research community have ignored rural lifelong learning. Nowadays there is very little policy discussion in government or debate amongst education researchers about rural lifelong learning. However the subject remains important, because – as this book seeks to demonstrate – lifelong learning can not only make a critical contribution to the lives of individuals and social groups living and working in the countryside but also help to address significant social, economic and political issues in rural areas.

All the contributions to the book have been written in the context of rural turmoil and transformation. The transition from the twentieth to twenty-first century has been marked by a rural Britain subjected to crisis after crisis. The mix includes the trauma of diseases such as BSE and Foot and Mouth; the decline in rural services and facilities, from the closure of banks to the withdrawal of buses; the influx of newcomers, often at the expense of local people, and the absence of affordable housing; rural social exclusion and marked income differentials; political controversy surrounding around the cost of fuel, genetically-modified crops, proposals to ban hunting, the right to roam and the designation and use of protected landscapes; and debates about subsidy, taxation and the role of the European Union in agricultural matters.

As some of these examples indicate, the crisis in rural Britain is also bound up with the complex impact of globalisation and capitalism on rural localities, with significant consequences for public attitudes towards the countryside. Nowadays, there is widespread doubt and major questions posed about the future of the countryside, certainly in contrast with how it is assumed to have existed in the recent past. The array of contemporary issues also reveals fundamental disagreements about rural places, people and society. These arguments are sometimes waged between people of the country and the city –

rural and metropolitan societies – but can also spring up between rural people. Indeed, ideas and notions of 'the country', 'the rural' and 'rurality' are complex, changing – over time and space – and often intensely contested.

Controversy about the countryside provided the media with one of the most newsworthy episodes in the 2001 British General Election campaign. During an electioneering visit to the Welsh seaside town of Rhyl, the Deputy Prime Minister, John Prescott, punched a protester who threw an egg at him. The event was seized on by the media as enlivening an otherwise dreary campaign and given massive national and international coverage. Although presented as the 'raw' and entertaining face of personality politics, with headlines such as 'John Prescott throws punch in scuffle', behind the story lay conflicts between urban and rural, mostly neglected by the media. It is tempting to see egg thrower and politician as warriors in the battle between rural and metropolitan. On the one hand, the egg thrower – one of a group of several dozen anti-government, pro-hunting, fuel-price-protesting rural demonstrators – was a young farm and hunt worker and representative of the key aspects of rural society. By contrast, the former seaman, trade-union activist and Ruskin College-educated politician, Member of Parliament for a northern city, was the urban, working-class voice of New Labour. Such an analysis, however, tends to ignore the complex relationships between rural and urban communities.

This complex and changing relationship is a theme examined by Raymond Williams in his powerful and influential critique, *The Country and the City*,[1] published three decades ago. Williams also argues against any simplistic reduction to a history of a golden but lost rural past. The argument is equally powerful today. Although contest, conflict, uncertainty about the future and the accelerating speed of change will remain persistent features of rural Britain, these should not be linked to an assumption that things were necessarily better in the past; that a once-golden age – the countryside as an Eden – has come to an end. In developing perspectives on lifelong learning in contemporary rural Britain, it is useful to both refute the notion of an idyllic rural past and to emphasise the significance of social, economic and political relationships between the country and other places in and beyond Britain.

Rural lifelong learning and the academy

The neglect of rural lifelong learning has various dimensions. Recent educational research, both theoretical and empirical, has eschewed the rural (although considerable attention has been focussed on the urban). The Economic and Social Research Council's major programme of research into 'the learning society' was silent on lifelong learning in rural areas.[2] The contributors to the annual Standing Conference on University Teaching and Research in the Education of Adults (SCUTREA) have rarely examined the rural dimensions of lifelong learning in the United Kingdom, with the most recent SCUTREA survey of the field appearing in 1974.[3]

The unfashionability of rural research within education has parallels in other subjects, including geography and sociology. One explanation is that 'the rural is a profoundly modernist category, and a profoundly modernist construction', which has fallen out of favour with the rise of postmodernism in the academy.[4] This is also related to how the rural is viewed and explained. Pratt usefully suggests: 'The positioning of the rural in society more generally has been paralleled (and I imply no stronger causal relation) by its marginalisation as an academic object of study.'[5]

The production of knowledge about rural continuing education (CE) and lifelong learning has typically been left to practitioners – to people working, organising and teaching in rural localities. One significant empirical contribution, funded by a CE research grant from the Universities' Funding Council in 1993, provides case studies of four localities and of the changing role of women in rural communities.[6] A key finding of this report is that 'many rural problems are practically "invisible" to national policymakers and this exacerbates a long history of under-provision.'[7] There have also been other, more recent accounts by practitioners working in rural lifelong learning, often reporting on specific localities or projects,[8] and a valuable NIACE practical guide to developing rural learning opportunities.[9]

As Bill Jones points out in Chapter Four, 'official' and government neglect of rural lifelong learning is evidenced by the absence of sustained discussion of the topic in the key lifelong learning reports of recent years.[10] Only very occasionally have these acknowledged the importance of rural lifelong learning. The influential 1997 Fryer Report, for example, asserts that for people living in 'relatively remote or far-flung places ... learning represents a point of contact, an opportunity for sociability and community building and an occasion in which people can review their own circumstances and priorities.'[11] There are two major problems with this approach. Firstly, and as many of the contributors to this volume emphasise, it belittles the significance of lifelong learning to suggest that it is primarily a mechanism for improving sociability and community building. Moreover, non-participation (and participation) in lifelong learning is clearly more than just a consequence of living in a remote or isolated community. Secondly, while the phrase 'remote or isolated communities' may be a precise and potentially technically useful formulation (for example, in allocating resources), it is less than satisfactory in arguing the political case for rural learners.

It is in such issues that the production of knowledge and the process of policy development and implementation intersect. The marginalisation of the rural in the lifelong learning and CE research agenda has meant that little or no knowledge has been gained to inform the production of policy. Learners and learning in rural localities have been marginalised. The absence of knowledge disempowers both individuals and communities. *Landscapes of Learning* is a contribution to placing rural lifelong learning back on the research, policy and political agendas.

Lifelong learning in rural policy

If 'rurality' and 'the rural' rarely enters into the heads of lifelong learning policy makers nowadays, it is equally alarming that those charged with developing rural policies have little to say about lifelong learning in the country. This is particularly apparent in the case of England, with the government's November 2000 White Paper, *Our Countryside: The Future – A Fair Deal for Rural England,* a prime example.[12] This tackles a diversity of matters, from rural services, housing, transport, social exclusion, farming, tourism, bio-diversity, planning and regeneration, crime and policing, wildlife and the natural environment. The emerging vision for rural England is of:

- A living *countryside, with thriving rural communities and access to high-quality services;*
- A working *countryside, with a diverse economy giving high and stable levels of employment;*
- A protected *countryside, in which the environment is sustained and enhanced, and which all can enjoy;*
- A vibrant *countryside, which can shape its own future and with its voice heard by government at all levels.*[13]

The accompanying aim is 'to sustain and enhance the distinctive environment, economy and social fabric of the English countryside for the benefit of all'. For a government so passionate about and committed to education, lifelong learning should surely feature prominently in realising the vision and aim of the White Paper. We would expect, for example, CE to be a key service towards helping rural communities to thrive; that vocational education would have an important role to play in improving rural job opportunities and developing the rural economy; that environmental education would contribute towards protecting the countryside; and, that education for citizenship would be a significant element in helping communities shape their own future and find their own voice.

However, the White Paper pays scant regard to lifelong learning and misses many opportunities to point out both the success stories and the potential of lifelong education and learning in rural areas. For example, the subject is virtually ignored in the sections on social exclusion and employment and income. In only one or two instances do the authors suggest a key role for lifelong learning. By far the most forceful statement is the following:

Improving education and learning opportunities for people throughout their lives is fundamental to our objectives for a globally competitive economy, a highly-skilled and productive workforce, equality of opportunity, the elimination of child poverty within one generation, and a better quality of life for all. This applies in rural as much as urban areas. We intend to make sure that people of all ages living in rural areas have full access to the range of opportunities available and that obstacles to access are addressed.[14]

At a first reading, this is a welcome vision of abundant and accessible rural lifelong learning opportunities for 'people of all ages', and not just for vocational reasons alone. Read more carefully, the statement is less positive. Barriers to access will be 'addressed', but not necessarily removed. And the phrase 'full access to the range of opportunities available' is meaningless if nothing is available. With the exception of online learning, using information and communications technology (ICT), the White Paper does not propose or see any need for an increase in rural adult learning provision.

To overcome the problem of distance between rural people and lifelong learning opportunities, the White Paper offers two solutions. First, it proclaims the benefits of distance learning, ICT, online courses and new technology, including the University for Industry (UfI), learndirect and 'e-Universities' projects. Second, it discusses helping poorer rural students with travel costs to the urban campuses.

Technology as the only or best way forward seems a curious argument when one of the barriers many rural people want to overcome is remote isolation. For many, the solution will not simply be to sit alone in front of a PC. And as a number of the contributors to this book demonstrate, on the basis of existing ICT learning projects in rural areas, there are complex issues to be tackled and unintended consequences to be encountered. At present ICT cannot be depended upon to provide equal lifelong opportunities for all; in practice, it too often compounds and refines existing inequalities. There are, of course, some success stories, but these usually depend on considerable and consistent on-the-ground support by dedicated tutors and ICT support staff.

Perhaps because of a belief in the salvation to be secured from ICT, the authors of the English Rural White Paper neglect the long-established success of higher and further education (HE and FE) providers and the voluntary adult education movement – including the Workers' Educational Association (WEA) – in taking courses to learners. As this book illustrates, venues are sometimes purpose-built adult education centres in rural towns, sometimes community colleges and schools, but often learners and teachers continue to meet in remote village and church halls. Providing learning opportunities in rural (and indeed urban) communities is the one sure way of getting to at least some of the most excluded and disadvantaged people, but the White Paper mostly eschews such policies. There are just a few brief mentions of, for example, the community use of schools for adult education (in some rural areas it has been occurring for decades) and innovative rural Adult and Community Learning Fund projects.

As this book seeks to argue, it should not be a choice between either new technology or face-to-face contact but, instead, both combined: accessible and supported new technologies, and opportunities to meet, discuss, debate and learn with other people. Interestingly, the separately-published White Paper Regional Case Studies do suggest the importance and vibrancy of rural adult learning.[15]

There are many other instances where rural report writers and policy makers neglect lifelong learning. The Countryside Agency proclaims that it provides a 'comprehensive analysis of the state of the [English] countryside' in its *State of the Countryside* annual reviews.[16] And yet there is no mention of rural lifelong learning in the review: it neither features as an indicator of 'community vibrancy,' nor in the section on education and training.

Early on in the White Paper it is asserted that rural 'opportunities for education and training are improving', although no supporting evidence is provided that this is true for adults.[17] The statement runs counter to the long-running funding problems which have led to the withdrawal of some HE and FE 'outreach' provisions over the last decade. For example, in Part One of this volume, Davidson, Ryley and Jones all comment on how new funding mechanisms for universities, mainstreaming and the developing quality agenda for HE have eroded the ability or desire of some HE institutions to maintain rural CE.

There are, of course, myriad definitional problems in using the term 'rural'. As the English Countryside Agency notes: 'While most people recognise countryside when they see it, deciding exactly what or where is 'rural' is difficult. There are many different definitions and classifications.'[18] Too often, definitions are based solely on administrative areas, thereby ignoring social and economic processes and relationships. Particular difficulties in defining the rural include the following:

- Separating rural and urban processes and localities from each other. This is often an impossible, unrewarding and perhaps unhelpful task because of the complex inter-relationships between the two. People might live in the country but work, shop, learn and play in the city or *vice versa*. In any event, rural areas may include quite large towns with some traditional urban problems.[19]
- The diversity of rural areas and conditions, making it difficult to ensure suitably sensitive approaches from region to region or for unique localities and communities.[20]
- The difficulty of identifying and measuring rural poverty, disadvantage and social exclusion when it is sometimes hidden amid relative wealth and prosperity. This point, emphasised by the contributors to this book, is one of the most significant conclusions from the Joseph Rowntree Foundation's *Action in Rural Areas* programme: 'Those experiencing social exclusion in rural areas are dispersed amongst apparent affluence, rather than concentrated together in problem areas. Area-based intervention may therefore be insufficient.'[21] The assumption that the majority or average characteristics apply to all in a geographical area is a fallacy identified by sociologists a century ago. It is still forgotten today when, for example, government and education funding councils target by postcode rather than individual and household characteristics.

Learning and the countryside

One of the useful concluding points made in the English Rural White Paper is that policies, of whatever character, should be subject to 'rural proofing'. This means that in developing and implementing new policies, policy makers should identify and assess the differential impact of policy in rural areas and consider what adjustments or compensations might be made to fit rural circumstances. Rural proofing may be usefully applied to education policies impacting on lifelong learning. In HE, for example, funding mechanisms for widening participation need to look beyond postcodes to identify rural needs and opportunities. Similarly, quality assurance regimes and processes might accept that the advantages of accessibility have sometimes to be set against lower – or at least different – standards of facilities and resources. Funding and planning systems for FE are currently evolving differently in Wales, Scotland and England, with consequent diverse implications for rural lifelong learning.

It is too soon to say, however, whether the policies of the Learning and Skills Council in England, with responsibility for FE funding and strategic planning, will be rurally proofed. The issue is partly about treating rural lifelong learning as seriously as, say, urban lifelong learning. This may involve treating it differently, rather than uniformly applying assumptions and policies that have been derived from and designed for other places or situations. It is noteworthy that some recent rural regeneration projects have drawn upon methods and ideas originally developed for urban contexts; a key to making a success of such projects will be to ensure they take account of the rural dimension.

CE professionals working in rural areas well know the ups and downs of adult learning in the countryside. On the one hand, the extent of demand for adult learning, much of it unfulfilled due to lack of resources; the under-represented groups; the myriad problems encountered by rural people trying to access learning opportunities; and the continual funding difficulties. On the other hand, the individual and community lifelong learning success stories, often against the odds; the success of many innovative FE and HE projects; and the often vibrant partnerships between voluntary and statutory providers. Partly because of past successes, but also because of its potential to change the lives of people and enhance communities, professionals working in the field (and it is easy to slip into rural metaphors) will agree that lifelong learning should be an essential part of policy for rural areas.

This is not to suggest, of course, that lifelong learning in rural communities is unproblematic. This book examines many of the issues and difficulties – some contextual and related to social and economic processes, and some practical, to do with resources and capacity – that beset rural learning. As already suggested, and for reasons discussed further by Ian Davidson in Chapter Two, the nature and purpose of present-day FE and HE often works against appropriate rural provision.[22] At other times, adult education itself becomes the 'problem'. In Chapter Four, for example, Bill Jones discusses how, in some villages, the struture of adult education may reflect a pastoral ideal implanted by urban middle-class village immigrants rather than a provision specifically designed for the rural community.

The issue of power exercised by dominant groups is discussed elsewhere in the book, extending to broader debates on the social relations, politics and practice of education and lifelong learning.[23] These concerns include the extent and circumstances in which education can, or cannot, change society or ameliorate structural inequalities. There are debates about the economic regeneration, social justice, community development and civic revival roles of education, and the balance between education for personal and cultural engagement, for social and political understanding and for vocational preparation.[24] Related issues include the difficulties encountered by excluded individuals and groups when accessing and using education, and the value of students defining and producing their own forms of knowledge.

For some people working within HE, recent widening participation activities have provided radical opportunities to 'stretch and turn' the academy and 're-theorise the discourse, influence the practice, operate dialectically and strategically within and against the systems in which we work.'[25] Most of the contributors to *Landscapes of Learning* do not adopt such an explicit political agenda. Nonetheless, in Part One they do provide contextual discussions that critically analyse the *status quo* and, in Part Two, detailed case studies of work with and for excluded and disadvantaged individuals and groups. In many of the case studies there is a strong theme of pragmatism; of attempting to ensure that, despite a series of constraints and limited resources, teaching, learning and guidance meets the needs and demands of excluded people. Faced with these challenges, some authors go on to describe how established and traditional approaches to pedagogy and curriculum can be re-defined or replaced with alternatives – sometimes by students (supported by tutors) generating their own agendas.

Landscapes of Learning is the product of work by the Rural Network of the Universities Association for Continuing Education (UACE). The network was first proposed in a rural session at the UACE annual conference in Swansea in 1995, with its first formal meeting being held in London in September 1996. The central aim of the network is to share experience and good practice in rural adult and continuing education. Although developing out of an HE organisation, the practitioner focus embraces all levels and forms of rural adult learning, from local voluntary groups to formal FE.

The importance of learning from shared experience is a principle theme of this book. Part One examines issues of geography, history, economy, culture and politics as they relate to rural areas and rural communities. Part Two provides eight case studies of lifelong learning in different rural localities in Wales, Scotland and England.

The wider context

In Chapter Two, Ian Davidson places United Kingdom rural society and CE in the context of globalisation and the emergence of more heavily-structured and top-down educational systems. He examines various representations of rural society, teasing out their relationships with cultural change, economic restructuring and 'the urban'. Place and space are used to explore how, in a global economy and society, rural communities may be marginal in oppressive or creative ways. Davidson then discusses how changes in educational policy and provision have decreased the freedom to respond to local needs and demands, with learning increasingly imposed on rural communities. He concludes by arguing that 'facework', and a curriculum that reflects local needs but with a global frame of reference, are both important if rural lifelong learning is to be socially inclusive. These last elements can be seen in practice in some of the case studies in Part Two.

Rural social exclusion provides the key concern for Peter Ryley in Chapter Three. Using many of the same conceptual tools as Davidson, Ryley describes the development of New Labour's lifelong learning policy, relating it to a 'new utilitarian agenda'. He examines economic and social change in the country; the restructuring of agriculture, the increasing importance of service-sector employment and at depletion of rural services. Processes of rural change are related to different types of rurality, based on region, locality and central versus peripheral areas. Local economies and social relationships are contrasted with implanted urban values, which leads to an examination of varieties of social exclusion – the young and the old, for example. The chapter concludes by arguing that lifelong learning will not succeed in a political vacuum. As with the other contributions, the substantive version of Chapter Three was completed in 2000 and before the crisis generated by the Foot and Mouth epidemic. And yet despite the impact of the epidemic, Ryley's analysis remains coherent and valuable.

In Chapter Four, Bill Jones provides a fascinating historical survey of rural adult education in Britain. His starting point is the educational life histories of some remarkable eighteenth-century rural working people, who against all the odds, gained 'a measure of learning'. The chapter goes on to chart the sometimes faltering development of organised rural adult education provision, noting how this varied from region to region and between Wales, Scotland and England. Beginning with the 1870 Education Act, influential reports and major pieces of government legislation and policy-making are shown to have had cumulative consequences for FE, HE and the provision made by local authorities and the voluntary sector. There was sometimes much opposition to rural adult education, especially from landowners and 'the village Establishment'. Nonetheless, a comprehensive system of provision for rural communities developed during the first six decades of the last century. But from the mid-1960s, and with the insidious blurring of rural-urban distinctions, the first signs were apparent that a watershed had been reached. 'Rural' became less exclusively significant in the analysis and organisation of provision, a trend that accelerated during the 1990s.

Case studies

The case studies in Part Two are diverse. The localities range from the relatively small scale (for example, Fenland villages [Chapter Ten] and two Border settlements [Chapter Eight]) to the large scale (including the south west as a region [Chapter Seven] and the Highlands and Islands [Chapter Eleven], which constitutes 20 per cent of the land-mass of the UK but contains one per cent of the population). Differing types and definitions of 'community' are used in the case studies, reflecting the contributors' awareness of the complexities and implications surrounding the use of the term.[26] The case studies also vary in subject matter. This ranges from adult guidance; the use of ICT in distance learning; developing ICT in rural villages; science provision; working with excluded older learners; the uses of oral history; partnerships with other providers; and the embryonic development of a radically new rural university.

Developing adult guidance in the sparsely-populated and low-income Mid and West Wales is the theme of Chapter Five. Sue Pester emphasises the critical role of guidance in working with excluded people – those least likely to access educational opportunities – using a holistic, client-centred approach. She reports on some practical guidance projects in the region and the use of the guidance process as a vehicle for developing skills. While noting some limitations, she stresses the benefits of adult guidance for socially excluded individuals and communities in rural areas.

John Nicholson, in Chapter Six, describes a project with the combined challenge of not only attracting people to take science courses but to do so in the context of rural East Anglia. Although the initial aim of the Science Starter Programme was to develop access and progression in rural areas, Nicholson emphasises the significant, wider benefits of an improved public understanding of science. The chapter examines the various problems encountered, the crucial role played by developing partnerships, and the delivery of an innovative, learner-centred curriculum. The difficulties of recruiting people to science courses were so great that tackling social exclusion was not a priority. Nicholson also describes the strategies used to disseminate the work beyond East Anglia and embed the programme once project funding ended. He concludes with a thoughtful appraisal of the successes and failures of the project.

Chapter Seven recounts the development of a distance learning programme using information technology (IT), emerging from the need to grapple with HE funding changes in rural south west England. The Learning Within Reach (LWR) programme described by Roseanne Benn succeeded in offering (in distance learning form) a growing proportion of the University of Exeter's part-time, award-bearing programmes, in recruiting and retaining students and maintaining the quality of the courses. Critical issues discussed by Benn include staff development, working with partnership organisations, and the often complex technical and support difficulties associated with distance learning. Although the LWR programme was aimed at countering the problems of access experienced by rural communities, an unlooked-for consequence was the recruitment of a more diverse group, including the housebound, carers and people with difficult working hours. Benn forcefully makes the point that IT distance learning may be very demanding for those students who need support with both study skills and technology, and that students without access to IT will continue to depend on paper-based study materials.

A different ICT project, in the remote Marches of Shropshire, is the subject of Chapter Eight by Len Graham and John O'Donoghue. Broadnet successfully established rural ICT resource centres. Through the delivery of local and flexible education and training opportunities for self-employed people, and small- and medium-sized enterprises, the project became involved in rural economic regeneration. The authors describe the development of 'electronic village halls', including one in a tiny hamlet of just 130 people (also functioning as a centre for the surrounding area) where the launch of the IT centre was a spectacular success, attracting 400 people. Graham and O'Donoghue argue that, despite its clear successes, the most obvious failures in the project arose from technical and support problems. Nonetheless, they argue that, in the long-term, ICT-based learning will be of major significance for adult learners in rural communities – empowering learners, enhancing provision, revitalising facilities and enabling social and economic regeneration.

In Chapter Nine, Marie Askham focuses on a project which developed university CE courses for older learners living in isolated areas in rural Bedfordshire and Hertfordshire. She describes the practicalities of planning and delivering the courses, building partnerships, student recruitment, developing an appropriate curriculum and assessing successes and failures. A key conclusion is the importance of selecting, training and supporting appropriate tutors. Another is identifying and meeting the needs of older learners; here an important strategy was to develop a selection of courses that drew heavily on local landscape and history for their subject matter. The project succeeded in encouraging the active participation of third-age learners in university CE. However Askham argues that short-term project work and funding is at odds with the open-ended, long-term embedding that is really required. She also points to low incomes and poor transport as underlying barriers to learning for many older people in rural areas.

Older learners also feature in Chapter Ten by Sue Oosthuizen, which describes an innovative oral history project in the Cambridgeshire Fens. A major challenge for this project was the 'defensive regional culture' of the Fens, with 'backwardness' often being used as a term to characterise the Fenland and its people. There were other inter-related problems of age, poverty and transport inadequacies. Oosthuizen describes how oral history was used as an androgogical tool; building on students' own experiences and allowing them to develop their personal and academic confidence. The chapter goes on to analyse the success of the project in widening participation, and especially in attracting older women with minimal formal educational qualifications. As with the previous chapter, issues of the time-consuming nature of development work, staff development, continuation funding and embedding are identified. The chapter concludes by arguing the case for the transformative and empowering force of liberal arts grounded within local culture in adult CE.

Chapter Eleven, by Jane Plenderleith and Veronica Adamson, discusses the establishment of a University of the Highlands and Islands (UHI) of Scotland – a huge land mass, and one of the least densely populated areas of Europe. This unique region is placed in the context of national and international processes, and the need to develop a radically different form of HE institution. This centres on plans to develop a rural curriculum – based on transferable skills rather than specific knowledge – that responds to the region's economic and social needs and aspirations, and to deliver it remotely through community learning networks linking people and places. The authors go on to examine challenges faced by the UHI project. These include those of social exclusion; meeting the needs of the significant minority ethnic population; the long-term, recurrent issues of adequate funding and the sustainability of the curriculum; the complexity of the university's federal structure; and the tension between the community focus of the project and its drive towards university status. Although of a different scale and character, these issues reflect many of the debates and arguments encountered in the other case studies. Since the chapter was completed there has been a fairly turbulent period in the history of the UHI. On 1 April 2001, the Scottish Parliament legally designated the UHI as a HE institution under the new name of the UHI Millennium Institute.

Widening participation in the North York Moors is the subject of the final chapter by Peter Ryley. Set in the context of the area's dual economy and complex pattern of rural social exclusion, this chapter addresses the development of working relationships and partnerships in a project designed to establish a 'University for the Moors'. Identifying gaps in provision and participation led to the production of a new curriculum, delivered by new teams of tutors and aimed at fostering economic, social and educational development. The four major elements discussed by Ryley are partnerships (especially with the voluntary sector); establishing new centres; ensuring a dispersed delivery (to counter the barriers created by rural geography); and facilitating open learning. As with other contributors to *Landscapes of Learning*, the author criticises short-term project funding: in this case 'the full period of funding had merely taken the project to the starting point.' In the concluding section of his chapter, Ryley moves from the specifics of the North York Moors to return to some of the more general concerns outlined in Part One of the volume. He discusses the logistic and social barriers to, and the role of higher education in, rural widening participation and the limited contribution education is able to make to decreasing polarisation in rural society.

A number of the case studies report on innovative rural projects, usually funded for short periods of time and many by the Higher Education Funding Council for England (HEFCE). As the authors demonstrate, the project funding led to some remarkably innovative and successful rural lifelong learning schemes, often financed with relatively small sums of money. But concerns are also raised about the inadequacies of time-limited, short-term, project funding and the difficulties of securing ongoing financial support (sometimes the work does not qualify for mainstream funding) and continuing and embedding the activity. At worst, former students and staff are left isolated and alone, with expectations raised but funding ended.

Despite the differences in geography and theme, some common threads can be drawn out of the case studies:

1. The importance of understanding both the specific rural locality and how it relates to the wider geographical context of the immediate region, the nation and the global economy.

2. Present-day lifelong learning policies are often inadequate in meeting the needs and demands of rural communities. To give just one example, many rural communities and individuals will be disadvantaged by the use of postcode analysis to distribute resources because it does not reveal the finely-grained nature of much rural disadvantage and social exclusion.

3. Making a success of rural lifelong learning depends on understanding and empowering rural learners as individuals and members of social groups, and also on staff possessing the relevant skills, knowledge and understanding. Staffing is part of a broader 'capacity' issue that involves ensuring that the resources (including ICT, the curriculum and venues) for lifelong learning are fit for the required purpose. The most certain successes occur when providers go to learners rather than *vice versa*.

4. Developing and implementing new educational policies and ways of delivering rural lifelong learning often have unintended and unexpected consequences. Sometimes, for example, the people accessing new rural learning opportunities are not those who were originally targeted.

5. Short-term project funding has both advantages and disadvantages. 'Soft' funding opens up new opportunities and may lead to excellent innovative work, but, too often, once funding ends the activity also ceases. The latter may be destructive to all involved and a prominent health warning should be placed on all invitations to bid for project funding. To twist the argument around, funding bodies need to ensure that mechanisms exist to enable successful and innovative work to be sustained and embedded once initial funding ceases. Equally

important, it is essential that the broader lessons of individual innovative projects are applied elsewhere. Good practice should be recognised and disseminated, while failures and unanticipated consequences – both to be expected with innovation and risk-taking – also need to be understood and publicised. HE and FE funding and planning bodies rarely have processes in place to replicate successful innovation.

6. There are seemingly intractable difficulties in ensuring that lifelong learning is accessible to all groups of rural people. While educational providers may know a great deal about people who do participate, we may never know just who decided not to join or take part, who was bypassed and excluded, and what, if anything, might have been done about it.

7. Partnerships are often critical to the success of rural lifelong learning. As Bill Jones indicates, this was true during much of the last century, and, as the case study contributors reveal, it remains true today. However, partnerships are rarely equal and usually need to be carefully and openly negotiated in order to be successful.[27]

8. Finally, many of the authors of this book also illustrate that, at its best, rural lifelong learning is embedded in the countryside (and often in a specific locality), albeit set within a broader regional, national or global context. The curriculum that works best relates closely to rural people and communities.

Landscapes of Learning is in part an appreciation of the strengths and successes of rural lifelong learning, often against considerable odds. It is also a challenge to policy-makers and educational researchers to treat rural lifelong learning as an important and significant subject, neglected for far too long.

Notes

1. Williams, R. (1973). *The Country and the City*. Chatto and Windus. Williams, as an Oxford University extra-mural tutor working in Sussex, was influential in the emergence and development of cultural studies. (See Steele, T. (1997). *The Emergence of Cultural Studies: Adult Education, Cultural Politics and the English Question*. Lawrence and Wishart.)

2. Coffield, F. ed. (2000). *Differing Visions of a Learning Society. Research Findings Volume 1*. Policy Press; and Coffield, F. ed. (2000). *Differing Visions of a Learning Society. Research Findings Volume 2*. Policy Press.

3. Styler, W.E. (1974). Research into rural adult education. Standing Conference on University Teaching and Research in the Education of Adults (SCUTREA), *Papers from the Fourth Annual Conference*. The 1999 SCUTREA conference theme was spaces and the education of adults and included a historical case study of rural adult education: Deacon, B. and

Thompson, L. Back to the land? Service and self-interest in adult education in rural England 1920–1945. In Merrill, B. ed. (1999). *The Final Frontier: Exploring Spaces in the Education of Adults.* SCUTREA; pp. 63–68.

4. Pratt, A.C. (1996). Deconstructing and reconstructing rural geographies. *Ecumene*; vol. 3, no. 3: pp. 345–50, quote p. 345.

5. *Ibid.*, p. 346.

6. Lowerson, J. and Thomson, A. eds. (1994). *Out of Sight, Out of Mind: Barriers to Participation in Rural Adult Education.* Centre for Continuing Education, the University of Sussex.

7. *Ibid.*, p. 2.

8. See, for example, the articles in issues 7 (October 1997) and 14 (March 2000) of *Ad Lib: Journal for Continuing Liberal Adult Education*, published by the University of Cambridge Board of Continuing Education, and articles in *Adults Learning* such as Lovett, T. (1997). Lifelong learning as a continuum. *Adults Learning*, April, pp. 214–16 and Tulett, C. (2001). Taking classes to the country. *Adults Learning*, October, pp. 27–29.

9. Payne, J. (2000). *Rural Learning: A Practical Guide to Developing Learning Opportunities in the Countryside.* NIACE.

10. Rural lifelong learning does not feature in the comprehensive review of adult learning in England. Hillage, J., Uden, T., Aldridge, F. and Eccles, J (2000). *Adult Learning in England: A Review.* IES Report 369, Institute for Employment Studies.

11. Advisory Group for Continuing Education and Lifelong Learning (1997). *Learning for the Twenty-first Century.* The Fryer Report, DfEE; p. 59.

12. *Our Countryside: The Future – A Fair Deal for Rural England.* DETR (2000). Cm 4909. (Also available at www.wildlife-countryside. detr.gov.uk.)

13. *Ibid.*, p. 6.

14. *Ibid.*, p. 36.

15. Regional case studies are available at www.wildlife-countryside. detr.gov.uk/ruralwp/regional.

16. The Countryside Agency (2001). *The State of the Countryside 2001.* The Countryside Agency.

17. *Op. cit.*, p. 9.

18. *Op. cit.*, p. 9.

19. *Regeneration Research Summary: Indices of Deprivation.* Number 31, DETR (2000). Also available at www.regeneration.detr.gov.uk.

20. *The State of the Countryside 2001* regional reports provide valuable indications of this spatial diversity and differentiation.

21. Quote from Joseph Rowntree Foundation (2000). Exclusive countryside? Social inclusion and regeneration in rural areas. *Foundations*; 760, p.1. See also the full report: Shucksmith, M. (2000). *Exclusive Countryside? Social*

Inclusion and Regeneration in Rural Areas. Joseph Rowntree Foundation.

22. See, also, the discussion of higher education in Thompson, J. ed. (2000). *Stretching the Academy.* NIACE.

23. *Ibid.*

24. This is discussed in Steele, T. (2000). Common goods: beyond the new work ethic to the universe of the imagination. in *Ibid.*, pp. 36–67.

25. *Ibid.*, p. 6.

26. See, for example, the discussions in Elliott, J., Francis, H., Humphreys, R., and Istance, D. (1996). *Communities and Their Universities. The Challenge of Lifelong Learning.* Lawrence and Wishart.

27. See also Joseph Rowntree Foundation (1999). Partnership working in rural regeneration. *Findings*; 039.

2

Rural society, social change and continuing education: from Wild Wales to the Aga Saga

Ian Davidson

Introduction

Rural society is located within an increasingly globalised society; continuing education (CE), in all its forms, is increasingly located within larger systems of education. Both rural society (and the communities that make it up) and CE are increasingly influenced by events outside their immediate location. This chapter brings together information from a variety of sources in order to reflect on the nature of rural communities and the role of CE within them. In particular, I reflect on the different ways in which educators working within rural areas can make sense of the rural; on the ways in which the rural might differ from the urban and the effect this might have on educational systems and processes.

The chapter is in four sections. The first gathers together some representations of rural society and comments on their place within contemporary culture. The second locates those representations within a strand of current social theory; the foregrounding of space and spatialisation of social and economic forms as a process of explaining and theorising social change and development. The third section lists and briefly discusses social and economic conditions within rural communities. The fourth describes some current developments in post-compulsory, adult CE and discusses the impact of these on rural educational provision.

Representations of the rural

The rurality of the ex-coal-mining valleys of South Wales and the scattered population of an agrarian Mid Wales would appear to have little in common. They would seem to have even less in common with the home-county villages of Surrey and Kent or the Highlands and Islands of Scotland. Within each area, within each village, there will be communities that exhibit striking differences, within a few miles or even within a few yards of each other. Individual rural communities themselves are not homogeneous. Neither are they static or easily represented.

Rurality has frequently been described as marginal, on the fringes of the metropolitan city and the nation state,[1] as the place where nothing happens and change is slow and distanced from the centres of power and commerce. Rural dialects were perceived to be inferior subsets of a standard language, the Celtic languages barbarous and uncivilised. Yet, conversely, it is in the rural that the strongest traces of national identity were, and probably are, often assumed to exist; a 'real' England in the villages of the Cotswolds or the leafy lanes of Kent; a 'real' Scotland in the Highlands and Islands; a 'real' Wales embodied in the hill farms of North and Mid Wales. It is in the rural that the traditions of a nation or a region are often assumed to be most clearly embodied, and that within these traditions there exists a rural or native wisdom, free of the artifice and superficial sophistication of the metropolis with its inevitable processes of commodification.

Modern consciousness of the rural (and its representations) maintains a mixed perspective: as a place of safety; a haven of retreat from the pressures of modern life; a place of brutal stupidity and want; as a place in which the 'real' people can be found; and a backwater which anyone with any common sense would want to leave. Many of the most pervasive views of the rural have been influenced by the Romantic period in literature and the publication of Wordsworth's *Lyrical Ballads*. The Romantic view of the rural was as a place of consolation from the pressures of industrial life, as morally uplifting and spiritually healing. It is axiomatic that, as processes of economic production changed from those which maintained the countryside in a relatively unchanging state to those which used up, destroyed and exploited natural resources, the rural should be increasingly seen as sublime or picturesque.

Literary representations of the rural population are particularly revealing. Often silent, they habitually form part of the picturesque landscape as they go about their work. From George Eliot to Enid Blyton's Five Find-Outers, countryfolk are indisputably 'other' – distinct from the situation of the author and his or her assumed readership. Occasionally given voice, they speak in barely distinguishable dialect; or they appear as the victim of some terrible tragedy, as an object of charity or to embody a kind of native wisdom. More contemporary representations through film and television continue these contradictions, whether through the idealised family life of *The Waltons*, the brutal backwoodsmen of *Deliverance* or the paranoia of *The Blair Witch Project*.

A brief and relatively random survey of contemporary political and policy statements reveals examples of varying attitudes to the rural. In the *Hansard* text of the House of Lords' debate from 11 March 1998 on Farming in Wales, Lord Hooson said: 'This is a time of real danger for the rural community [*note the singular and the definite article*]. I am talking about an area which is the backbone of Welsh cultural and social life.'[2]

In the same debate Lord Kenyon listed his paradigm of rurality and the impact of change upon it:

> *I am fortunate to live in a rural village which still boasts a church, albeit with a falling congregation, a sub-post office and general store, a garage, a butcher's shop and a pub. But all around me I see the shutters going up in businesses as they are forced to close from lack of customers … At the same time we have an exodus of the young blood from the rural communities. The bright lights of the cities beckon them and they follow that star.[3]*

In the supplementary guidance to Rural Development Agencies provided by the Department of the Environment Transport and the Regions,[4] rurality is defined as 'wards which lie outside the boundaries of settlements of 10,000 or greater population' and whose particular features are 'sparsity of population, small settlements of narrow economic base, relative inaccessibility, remoteness and peripharility.' It refers to a 'living' and 'working' countryside but recognises the interdependence of town and country, desires a countryside in which the historic and natural environment is protected and enhanced with 'genuine' access for all.

The countryside is therefore a spectacle, a sight to be enjoyed (consumed), as well as a site of economic activity. Importantly, and this rings true for those working in rural CE, the Rural Development Agencies recognise that 'the pursuit of business efficiency objectives may lead organisations to cut back on their outreach work in rural areas, which may intensify the problems of socially excluded individuals or deprived neighbourhoods'.

A discussion paper produced by the National Rural Enterprise Centre[5] problematises the rural by producing a list of negatives. Examples of these are:

- 75 per cent of villages have no daily bus service
- 74 per cent of rural parishes have no GP
- 91 per cent of villages have no bank or building society.

This list of negatives is prefaced by the following statement: 'It is fundamental that wherever people live they should have the same rights of access to basic services such as education and health care, retail services, libraries, information, advice and government services.'

It is tempting to agree. Yet in contradiction, the 1989 Gallup Survey quoted by Hallacree[6] suggests people prefer a rural residential environment for peace and quiet, the feeling of space, where less change appears to have taken place and they feel more in touch with their past – and, overwhelmingly, with nature. It is common statistical sense that isolated rural communities cannot support the same range of services, either governmental or commercial, as a large urban population. Bland solutions – which suggest that an equality (and equal quality) of access can be provided by a couple of computers available after hours in the local school or the post office – should also be avoided. None of which is to suggest that the rural population should accept a second-class service, grateful for any crumbs that fall off the table of their nearest urban conurbation. Nor that information and communication technologies do not have a very important

21

part to play in providing access to a wider world. Neither would I want to deny that poverty, unemployment or a range of other social ills exist within rural communities. There are the same cultural reasons why sectors of the rural population, particularly those with a negative experience of education and employment, will fail to access services, including education, as exist in urban areas. Mere accessibility or equality of opportunity (which implies that everyone is coming from the same place and is equally culturally able to take advantage of those opportunities) will be inadequate. It has to be reinforced by a process of intervention that relates to the context in which it is operating, whether that intervention arises from outside the community or from within it.

Moreover, producing lists of what the rural doesn't have from an apparent urban perspective distracts attention from the cultural and social context of the rural. Without wishing to reduce the rural to a list of commodities to stack up against the attraction of the urban, those characteristics in the Gallup survey quoted above – as well as Sherwood's list,[7] which includes 'quietness', 'friendliness', 'village life' and 'natural' surroundings – are all resources which are perceived to be available to those that live in the countryside. Underlying a number of responses would appear to be the advantages of living in a small community. Rural people perceive themselves as more self-reliant and better able to depend on their neighbours. Extended family units are often geographically close to each other. Small farms are one of the few places where the family still forms the main economic unit, thereby providing (favourable circumstances allowing) stability and security. There is more of a sense of long-standing community than in many urban areas.

I do not want to fall into the trap of romanticising the countryside, but neither do I want to over-problematise it. Nor would I suggest that many features of rural life cannot be found in urban life. I would, however, be critical of descriptions of the rural and the people who live in it, as a series of problems which need solving (because rural areas do not offer the same, or as many, facilities as urban areas), whether through 'outside' intervention or from developing capacities within communities. I would also question the liberal assertion, rapidly becoming received wisdom, that positive change in rural communities can only arise from within and that external influences are always destructive and disempowering. In many cases it is the 'irritant' from outside the community that proves to be the catalyst for change.

All of this leads me to the slightly uncomfortable conclusion that there is something specific about the rural and rural communities, however difficult that may be to define. This is not in simple opposition to the urban, nor the false consciousness of a rural paradigm of thatched cottages and the sound of willow on leather. The differences will be contextually specific and each attempt to generalise will lead to a list of exemptions from the rule. However it does mean that educators working in rural areas need to be alert to the range of internal and external pressures and processes which simultaneously splinter and bring together communities within a rural context.

The rural is therefore a contested site. There is no common perspective, no simple form of representation, be it Thomas Hardy's Wessex, *Last of the Summer Wine*, *Pobl y Cwm* or *Dr. Finlay's Casebook*. In *Keywords*, Raymond Williams[8] usefully traces the genealogy of 'country' (as in countryside) back to '*contrata terra* meaning land "lying opposite, over against or facing". The rural, or the country, from that definition, is that which you see before you, not that which surrounds you; it is something which you enter.

Absent others

To try to pin down what rural *really* means to a late-modern world appears an impossible task. To the mountain-climbers and hang-gliders it is a place of danger and risk; to the visiting motorist it is a spectacle which unfolds outside the windscreen. Yet it would be too easy to increasingly view the countryside as a kind of simulacrum: a simulated representation, best embodied in a theme-park world as a collection of signs – grass, trees, thatched cottages, etc. The countryside is also a place of memory (both personal and communal) and a place of tradition resistant to change. The rural was never timeless and tranquil, but a place of work and living as well as rest and retreat.

Since the industrial revolution, and through modernity to post- or late-modernity, the impact of national and global communications networks linking the rural to the urban has been an implacable process. The mass availability of telephone, radio and television, better road networks and rail links (but often poorer local public transport) have shrunk the distance between the rural and the urban for those with the resources to travel. Responding to and reflecting such changes, recent social theory – and particularly human and social geography[9] – seeks to explain the development of late or post-modernity by foregrounding the spatial factors, alongside the historical, which construct contemporary society and culture:

> The great obsession of the nineteenth century was, as we know, history: with its themes of development and suspension, of crisis and cycle, themes of the ever accumulating past, with its preponderance of dead men and the menacing glaciation of the world … The present epoch will perhaps be, above all, the epoch of space. We are in the epoch of simultaneity: we are in the epoch of juxtaposition, the epoch of the near and far, of the side by side, of the dispersed. We are at a moment, I believe, when our experience of the world is less that of a long life developing through time than that of a network that connects points and intersects with its own skein.[10]

Frederic Jameson refers to:

> spatial peculiarities of postmodernism as symptoms and expressions of a new and historically original dilemma, one that involves our insertion as individual subjects into a multidimensional set of radically discontinuous realities, whose frames range from the still surviving spaces of bourgeois private life all the way to the unimaginable decentering of global capitalism itself.[11]

During the early twenty-first century, historical reference points have merged with contemporaneous realities. People can no longer live in a continuum marked out by the lives of their families and neighbours, but must survive (and, in some cases, thrive) within a range of different sets of experience, each one merging and overlapping. A sense of rural history has been instrumental in making sense of change and development. Jameson is suggesting (although with trepidation) that our sense of ourselves and our communities, and the ways we represent these to ourselves and to others, exist within multiple and overlapping realities that defy both logic and closure. A consequence of this is '...the enormous strategic and tactical difficulties of co-ordinating local and grassroots or neighbourhood political actions with national or international ones.'[12]

Anthony Giddens in *The Consequences of Modernity* makes a useful distinction between place and space where place is the 'locale', a place of personal history, family engagements, 'dominated by presence.' Modernity, according to Giddens, 'increasingly tears space away from place by fostering relations between absent others.'[13] Space, crudely globalised forces and abstract systems, has an increasing impact on place. It is in the countryside, where the undisturbed locale of memory and tradition could still appear to exist, that 'space and place largely co-exist.' Such a view is increasingly difficult to maintain.

The consequences of an increasingly spatialised society are too many to list and, in many ways, cannot be adequately charted during a process of very rapid change in both knowledge production and transmission and the increasing globalisation of economic forces. It certainly means that the flawed notion of the rural, as distanced from the creative and destructive forces of global capitalism and subsequent commodification of public and private spheres of life, cannot be sustained. The rural is increasingly affected by, and in turn will influence those changes which in previous times would mostly have been seen as urban in nature and consequence. It should also mean that the benefits of a global society will become increasingly available to those living in rural areas.

The growing impact of global systems would appear to lead to the conclusion that there is no meaningful distinction between the rural and the urban; that the world is a vast network and the rural is merely a geographically peripheral part of a population. In an age of mass electronic communication and improved transport systems, individuals are decreasingly fixed – physically or conceptually – within their locale and will form connections with distant others through common interests. Yet, alternatively, there is now considerable interest in the regional and local (particularly the idea of community) as a counter to the process of globalisation. From the 1960s onwards, more people have actively chosen to live in rural areas. There is also a growing market in regional and ethnic culture and products as counters to the global and the mass-produced.

The ideas relating to the concept of community are complex and often contradictory and I do not intend to trace the genealogy of the term. I would, however, like to use a quote from *Reading Rosehill*, by George Revill, which, although describing an urban community, is a useful guideline for those engaged in community development activity. He states:

> *The value of community as a concept ... is that it throws into prominence the tensions between senses of belonging which form ties between individuals and groups and between peoples and places. It is not that it enables us to identify a stable or even dominant set of social and cultural characteristics by which a particular place or group might be identified. Rather, community focuses interest on the processes that create a sense of stability from a contested terrain in which versions of place and notions of identity are supported by different groups and individuals with varying powers to articulate their positions.*[14]

A community exists, therefore, not as a culturally or ideologically homogenous group, but as a process in which those who find themselves within a locale moreorless come together out of a common interest. It may well be made up of those who both live and work within the locale, those who have chosen to live within a particular location yet work away and those who have retired to the countryside for an improved quality of life. Some issues may bring them together; others may drive them apart. Revill is claiming – and I think this is a useful concept for those who seek to provide CE in rural communities – that what binds a community is a shared involvement (which might mean detachment or explicit criticism) in the processes of developing a sense of community, rather than a set of common rural values. This is not a process that will produce a future, perfectly-formed rural utopia, but one that is ongoing and without closure.

Bell Hooks, writing in *Yearning: Race, Gender and Cultural Politics*, usefully reminds us that: 'There is a definite distinction between the marginality which is imposed by oppressive structure and that marginality one chooses as a site of resistance, a location of radical openness and possibility.'[15]

In *Contested Countryside Cultures*,[16] a range of authors refer to the countryside as a place in which radical alternatives can be developed and where attitudes towards gender, sexual preference and economic activity within global capitalism can be explored. The distinction between marginality as a form of social exclusion or oppression, or as a site of creativity, must always be borne in mind in any discussion about adult CE in rural locations. Those working in the rural, whether entering it from a distant centre to provide services or working from within a rural community, must operate within the tension of being both coloniser and creator of a rural space. They are both part of a system which might seek to control behaviour (however well intentioned that control, or beneficial its results) and promote the values of the nation state, and creators of potential sites of resistance.

A problematic rural

As the rural becomes increasingly viewed as a commodity to be simultaneously consumed and preserved, inhabitation of it becomes problematical. In *Working with Rural Communities*, Francis and Henderson[17] list a number of rural trends and problems affecting rural people:

1. There have been significant population shifts between the town and the country. Although, in many cases, the population in rural areas may have remained static, this disguises relatively well-off urban dwellers (including those of retirement age) moving into the countryside and displacing the rural working class. Developments in information and communication technologies (ICT), and thereby the ability of people to work from home, will only exacerbate this problem. In various areas of 'outstanding natural beauty' there has also been a significant increase in second-home ownership, with its concomitant negative impact on the structure of the local community and the affordability of houses for those who work locally.

2. The employment structure in rural areas has radically altered as traditional rural industries either cease to operate or become increasingly mechanised. The impact of these changes – affecting industries such as agriculture, fishing and quarrying – is often the cause of population shifts, resulting in significant changes to the physical and cultural make-up of rural communities.

3. There has been a decline of public services in rural areas which is mirrored by the increasing non-viability of other services, such as local shops or pubs. This creates inequality; those without personal transport or on low incomes are most greatly affected by both a lack of local amenities and a decrease in the availability of public transport.

4. There is a perceived erosion of rural culture. Francis and Henderson refer to 'a challenge to long-held and deeply-rooted values.' While such values would probably be very difficult to finally locate within a heterogeneous rural community, recent calls to preserve the countryside and the rural way of life come from the landed gentry, those who use the countryside for recreation, those who live and work there and those concerned with 'environmental' issues (while accepting that all these attributes may be present in one person). The degree to which a Cornish fisherman (unable to afford to live in a fisherman's cottage and now living in social housing some distance from the shore), the owner of a large estate in East Anglia and those choosing to live an alternative lifestyle on a small holding in Mid Wales might share 'deeply rooted values' is highly debatable. Yet they are all, in some way, part of the rural.

Any consideration of rural post-compulsory education (and that juxtaposition of terms seems to jar) must acknowledge the differing realities and views of the rural – the view from the city ramparts or the view from over the hedge. Equally, the set of assumptions, nostalgias and attitudes inherited from previous generations and developed through literary, filmic and mass media representations of the rural should be taken into account.

The imposition of learning

Similarly, modern forms of adult CE, at a time of considerable upheaval within educational institutions, have difficulty identifying a common set of dependable values or activities. The curriculum exhibits both conservatism and radicalism, linked to traditionalism and occasional hyper-modernity, in its forms of delivery. Any attempt to define current developments in adult CE leads one into a maze of contradictory policies, theoretical positions and practical realities.

Over the past three decades there has been considerable development of more flexible modes of delivery in post-compulsory education. These changes are justified in the interest of providing equality of opportunity and access to educational provision for all members of society, as well as through the discourse of consumer choice. They would appear to be particularly relevant to those providing rural CE, allowing, through systems of credit accumulation and transfer, access to flexibly delivered modules which carry credit towards qualifications to those distanced from the urban centres of delivery.

The Access 'movement',[18] which, during the 1990s, developed close ties with credit developments (and, to some extent, was subsumed by them), aimed to right a perceived social injustice: namely that higher education (HE) was disproportionately beneficial to those children of middle-class families. It developed a validated national system of Access courses (now under the auspices of the Quality Assurance Agency) as a third route into HE, alongside A-levels and vocational qualifications. The National Open College Network is now the main accreditational body for adult students. It is made up of a number of autonomous regional networks through which the vast majority of Access to HE courses are now accredited. There is now talk of providing an 'open' system of credit accumulation and transfer, whereby 'learners' can accumulate credits over a period of time at a pace which suits their needs. Learning, so the story goes, can be accredited whenever and wherever it takes place: in the workplace, through the involvement of individuals with voluntary organisations or within educational establishments.

The accreditation of learning accelerated during the 1990s, following the Further and Higher Education Act of 1992. This stipulated that in order to qualify for funding, courses must prepare students for progression to formal qualification bearing provision. The consequence was a mass of activity involving the accreditation of previously non-accredited provision (sometimes referred to as leisure courses) at both further education (FE) and HE levels. This, in turn, led to the creation of progression frameworks to encourage student movement from informal into more formal education, leading to qualifications.

There are differing perspectives on the accreditation of learning. On the one hand, it can be seen as a process that provides equal opportunity to all learners, thereby giving them standing within society and the educational system. On the other hand, it can be seen as a process of commodification – of usurping the 'free space' of learning through bureaucratic procedures of assessment and quality assurance.

Whilst the development of more flexible FE has gathered momentum (particularly to serve the needs of industry and those in employment), the situation in HE has been more complex. The 1992 Act removed the binary line between 'traditional' universities and former polytechnics, creating a much enlarged and homogeneous HE sector. Consequently, institutions with widely differing missions and methods of operation have been brought together – from ancient universities that focus on international research, to teaching institutions with a regional or vocational mission. Curricula now vary from highly-structured, full-time degree courses to flexible, combined-studies degrees, delivered both full- and part-time.

The most significant change for rural areas has been the mainstreaming of extra-mural or CE provision. The traditional model of extra-mural provision normally involved a separate section of the university being given responsibility to take learning outside the walls of the university and into the local population. The history of extra-mural provision is well documented elsewhere.[19] Crudely, however, it involved delivering courses through series of lectures in towns and villages within a defined geographical area. Many extra-mural departments worked closely with the local branch of the Workers' Educational Association (WEA) to the extent where their work, from the perspective of the student, was often indistinguishable. Mainstreaming involved bringing all courses – full- or part-time, on- or off-campus – into the main qualifications framework of the institution, if they were to qualify for continued funding.

Following the mainstreaming process, both the WEA in the FE sector, and the departments of extra-mural studies in the HE sector, were expected to play a major part in the process of widening access to education to those least likely to take part. One such group was those communities and individuals perceived to be disadvantaged by geography. To be educationally, and therefore socially excluded because of their distance from the centres of learning was considered unacceptable in a developed, industrial country.

Critics, as I mentioned earlier, have seen systems of credit accumulation and transfer as an important part of the commodification of learning. There are numerous way in which learning has become increasingly commodified, through evolving into abstract systems which seek to colonise the concrete space of individual and community life. The application of systems of credit (itself a term borrowed from the financial sector) and modularisation (a term used to describe production processes) have an unavoidable relationship to economic development. The arguments surrounding the economic value of learning, both to the individual and the nation state, have been made both by those who 'manage' the economy and by those working within the educational system itself. Such arguments are not new, but they have recently come into sharp focus in an attempt to persuade students that the fees for their qualifications are a worthwhile investment. A 'user-friendly' delivery of learning (at a time and a place to suit the student) reflects the more flexible delivery of other services, particularly those in the retail and financial sectors. This new paradigm for education, which confers an economic value within a market place, is riven by contradiction – not least of which is the individual motivation of students. It also creates new cohorts of the socially excluded; those who, for reason of age, are not economically active. There is, however, an increasingly critical mass of opinion to support flexible, credit-based learning, linked to economic need, from both the free marketeers on the Right and those on the Left who seek to develop a more equal society through providing equality of opportunity.

The development of services for rural locations is seen by government and local authorities as critical in the drive to draw in the socially excluded. Within the constraints of current economic thinking, the answer to providing access to services and education is perceived as best carried out through multi-agency activity (thereby bringing about both synergy and cost effectiveness) and strongly dependent on the use of ICT. This is well theorised in the work of Beck, Giddens and Lash[20] who underline the implications of trust and risk in a society in which power and authority are no longer vested in a place (for example, a university or bank manager's office) but in abstract systems (of which a credit-based education system is one).

The use of new technologies in the delivery of education to rural areas creates tensions. Putting aside the issues of the physical and cultural access to the hardware required, the delivery of information through multiple access points results in homogenisation of the curriculum. Rural adult education has often sought to draw on the specific features of a locality, its local history, geographical or social features or industrial processes. Latterly, it has frequently focussed on providing for the needs of the community. A curriculum, developed at a centre of learning (a university, for example), for remote delivery using common resources, will necessarily contain an element of standardisation. The monitoring of standards of achievement through an assessment process will exacerbate this standardisation. Both elements, taken alongside the lack of facework through the use of new technologies, will work against the development of a curriculum tailored to a particular locality. Contradictorily, it is often through the use of a curriculum designed with a particular group in mind or, designed with the group themselves, that those least likely to take part in mainstream educational provision can be encouraged to participate.

In short, a series of issues and tensions arise when institutions seek to develop provision in rural areas. Modularised and credit-based curricula provide the mechanisms whereby small sections of courses can be shipped out to remote areas, but the larger, qualification-bearing courses are more difficult to adapt to the specific context of the place of delivery. These demand increased resources and student support, both of which tend to shift the location of courses away from peripheral areas and into the centre. Whilst the development of distance-learning provision and the use of ICT provide the means for remote delivery, these lack the necessary face-to-face contact and personal involvement which can encourage participation in those groups least likely to take part in any educational provision. The evidence[21] seems to suggest that merely distributing educational opportunities more widely, but without a strategy of intervention, will only succeed in recruiting more of those social groups who already take part. The nature of such intervention cannot be forecast, either in the short- or the long-term; it will relate to the particular context in which it takes place. However, it will need to be reflexive; to change as the circumstances of the community change, due to the internal and external forces acting upon it.

Conclusions

These conclusions are tentative. This chapter has brought together information and ideas from a number of sources in order to reflect on contemporary concepts of the rural, and the role that adult CE can have within rural areas. The focus of modernist and post-modern social theory is on the urban[22] and the way in which, over the last two decades, an understanding of the social construction of space (particularly urban space) can reveal sources of oppression. As the increasingly rapid change of pace in urban society delivers a more fruitful area of research, this becomes more predictable. For those working with rural communities, it is perhaps useful to reflect on Harvey's statement that: 'As spatial barriers diminish so we become much more sensitised to what the world's spaces contain.'[23]

For the educational practitioner within a rural context, increased spatialisation of social and economic structures has many implications. Within a multi-national industry, fellow workers will not only be those in the same work place but also those working for the same employer across the globe. The owner of a small farm on marginal land may have as much in common with farmers in the American Mid West as those in his immediate locality. Community education workers may therefore benefit from links which are both local and international. This is indeed crucial if, as Jameson says, 'the truth of experience no longer coincides with the place in which it takes place.'[24]

While education may be provided within a local context, its role may be not only to help people in locating themselves historically within their own locality but also within a range of regional, national and international communities. The education may be local but the frame of reference global; explanations of the individual and communal condition may well come from a combination of examining the historical conditions that brought about their community and also its construction within a range of contemporaneous international spaces.

The role of rural educationalists will be to draw on individual and communal histories and traditions, and to integrate these elements – through the content of courses and the context of delivery – within a broader understanding of those global and local forces which construct the spaces we all inhabit.

Notes

1. See Williams, R. (1973). *The Country and the City*. Chatto and Windus, (amongst others).
2. Lords *Hansard* text. 11 March 1998: http://www.parliament.
3. Lords *Hansard* text. 11 March 1998: http://www.parliament.
4. UK DETR: http://www.local-regions.detr.gov.uk.
5. *Vision for the Future of Rural Services* (1998) National Rural Enterprise Centre.
6. Halfacree, K. (1997). Contesting roles for the post-productivist countryside. In Cloke, P.J. and Little, J. eds. *Contested Countryside Cultures*. Routledge; p. 75.
7. *Ibid.*, p. 76.
8. William, R. (1976). *Keywords*. Fontana.
9. See the work of Henri Lefebvre, Edward Soja and Derek Gregory amongst others.
10. Foucault, M. quoted in Soja, E. (1995). Heterotopologies. In Watson, S. and Gibson, K. eds. *Postmodern Cities and Spaces*. Blackwell; p. 17.
11. Jameson, F. (1988). 'Cognitive Mapping'. In Nelson, C. and Grossberg, L. eds. *Marxism and the Interpretation of Culture*. Urbana.
12. *Ibid*.
13. Giddens, A. (1990). *The Consequences of Modernity*. Polity Press; p. 18.
14. George Revill (1993). Reading Rosehill. In Keith, M. and Pile, S. eds. *Place and the Politics of Identity*. Routledge; p. 120.
15. Bell Hooks quoted by Soja, E. (1997). *Planning in/for postmodernity*. In Benko, G. and Stromhayer, U. eds. *Space and Social Theory*, Blackwell; p. 247.
16. Cloke and Little, *op. cit.*
17. Francis, D. and Henderson, P. (1992). *Working with Rural Communities*. Macmillan.
18. See, for example, Davies, P. and Parry, G. (1993). *Recognising Access*. NIACE.
19. See, for example, Fieldhouse, R. *et al.* (1996). *A History of Modern British Adult Education*. NIACE.
20. Beck, U. Giddens, A. and Lash, S. (1994). *Reflexive Modernization*. Polity Press.
21. Sargant, N. *et al.* (1997). *The Learning Divide*. NIACE.
22. Harvey, D. (1990). *The Condition of Postmodernity*. Blackwell.
23. *Ibid.*, p. 295.
24. Jameson, quoted in Harvey, *ibid.*, p. 261.

3

Social exclusion and lifelong learning in rural areas

Peter Ryley

Introduction

This Government is committed to the establishment of a learning society in which all people have opportunities to succeed. Increasing access to learning and providing opportunities for success and progression are fundamental to the Government's strategy. These are the keys to social cohesion and success.

DfEE (1998), Further Education for the New Millennium

With these words, the government marked a major policy shift. Lifelong learning was to move from the margins to a more central place in the rhetoric, at least, of educational policy makers. Furthermore it was now to be seen as a vital part of programmes of social reform addressed at promoting 'social inclusion'. Some of these programmes have been clustered under the generic title of the New Deal. The terminology may be from F. D. Roosevelt but the policy is closer to Clinton, with its emphasis on 'welfare to work'. Funded initially by a windfall tax on privatised utilities, it started as a near-compulsory training and work-placement scheme for the under-25s. It has now been extended to older people, the over-50s, lone parents and the disabled. At its heart is the supply-side concept of human capital: that economic prosperity depends on the development of skills in the workforce.

As is often the case with New Labour, there was a lack of clarity at the centre of the policy to make it appear consensual. The Right, whilst still disapproving of the social interventionism of the 'New Deal', could still see this as balancing rights with responsibilities; encouraging learning as part of individuals' self-improvement and a way of taking personal responsibility for lifting themselves from poverty. Left-leaning cynics (including this author) deplored the sense that this is yet another moral duty to be imposed upon the poor to compensate for the 'sin' of their poverty, but were still enthused by the possibilities. The new utilitarian agenda meant that lifelong learning could now take its place as part of a drive towards greater social equality. Whilst traditional liberal justifications, emphasising personal and communal development, were relegated in importance, 'social purpose education' fits neatly with the idea of learning as a tool to promote 'social cohesion'.

But what of *rural* continuing education (CE)? Given the stereotypical views of both the countryside and social deprivation, it would seem that urban, inner-city concerns were to be at the forefront of policy. However, social exclusion is not a prerogative of the town. It is a feature of rural life – and an understanding of the processes is a prerequisite for the development of rural CE. Despite this, the prevalent vision of rural society does not include disadvantage. Romanticism still dominates the popular imagination, despite the growth of rural pressure politics. This chapter aims to explore the nature of rural social exclusion – not only to illustrate its existence, but to emphasise the distinctive nature of social disadvantage in the countryside. It is only through such an understanding that rural CE can address the new agenda and develop a coherent policy of lifelong learning.

Politics and the countryside

The difficulty in viewing rural areas as a site of social conflict is graphically demonstrated by one of the most curious features of the 1998 Countryside March in London: the response of the Left. The Countryside March was the product of the first specifically rural British campaign group, the Countryside Alliance. The Alliance had been formed to fight the, then, new Labour government's pledge to ban hunting with hounds. However, it rallied wider rural concerns and forced its way on to the political agenda with a large-scale demonstration in the capital city. The Liberal press was broadly hostile, choosing to focus on the hunting issue alone. Steve Bell's *Guardian* cartoons, so often the highlight of the week, depicted a procession led by a greedy, bloodthirsty, Barbour-clad élite which slowly degenerated into ranks peopled by some form of primitive throwback.[1] There could scarcely have been a more vivid example of urban prejudice. *The Observer* was more measured but also tried to discredit the march. It talked of 'class war in the countryside'[2] and portrayed the marchers as being pressurised by the landed interest. There may well have been a gulf between the interests of the leadership and participants, but the fact that people demonstrated in such numbers signified that all is not well in rural Britain.

It was quite clear that the Countryside Alliance itself was a conservative organisation seeking to preserve the rural balance of power. But, however opportunistic it may have been, it succeeded in mobilising those whose usual sympathies would not normally lie with the leadership. What should have concerned both the government and the Left is that the support for the march signalled serious weaknesses in the rural economy. The early incoherence of the rural sentiment embodied in the first march subsequently became more targeted. In 1999 and 2000 New Labour revitalised the movement by reviving the prospect of anti-hunting legislation after initially appearing to kill Mike Foster's Private

Member's Bill. Whilst blood sports remained the main *raison d'être* of the Alliance, it also sought to capitalise on broader discontents by launching campaigns to preserve rural post offices and establishing The Campaign for Independent Food.[3]

Rural discontent was further highlighted by the extraordinary emergence of direct action in British politics through the fuel crisis. In September 2000, the country's road transport network was brought to the edge of collapse by the blockade of oil refineries by a combination of farmers and road hauliers protesting about high fuel taxes. The media spotlight was placed on the leadership offered, and the rivalry between, two leading figures: the North-Wales hill farmer, Brynle Williams, and Monmouth dairy farmer, David Handley, the chairman of the People's Fuel Lobby. Again, the metropolitan Left was caustic, often failing to distinguish this small-business protest from the corporate road lobby. If the crisis demonstrated anything, it was the vulnerability of agriculture and small businesses to rising fixed costs – in this case, partly caused by the use of indirect taxation as a revenue source to enable income tax to be held steady and corporate taxation lowered.

The protests and the persistence of the Alliance, with its slow development away from being a single-issue group, are indicators of the existence of structural rural disadvantage. Such disadvantage shares many common features with that in urban areas, but is exacerbated by the rural nature of its setting – and there are issues specific to the countryside

The Third Way

Until the advent of Thatcherism, a discussion of inequality would have been synonymous with class. But New Labour has also argued for the redundancy of the term and a class analysis is now anathema. As a result, 'social exclusion' has become dominant. This marks a substantial conceptual shift. John Smith's leadership established the Commission on *Social Justice* (my emphasis), implying economic rights. New Labour seeks to balance rights and responsibilities and thus changes the role of government to one of providing an infrastructure in which individuals can take responsibility for using the life chances provided, rather than one which structurally excludes them from all opportunities. Anthony Giddens, in a seminal New Labour text, *The Third Way*, clarifies this thinking:

> *The new politics defines equality as inclusion and inequality as exclusion, although these terms need some spelling out. Inclusion refers in the broadest sense to citizenship, to the civil and political rights and obligations that all members of a society should have, not just formally, but as a reality of their lives. It also refers to opportunities and to involvement in public space. In a society where work remains central to self-esteem and standard of living, access to work is one main context of opportunity. Education is another, and would be so even if it weren't so important for the employment possibilities to which it is relevant.[4]*

Although ostensibly arguing against neo-liberal meritocratic ideology, Giddens repositions his argument on equality far closer to that model than he would care to admit when he writes that 'recent discussions amongst social democrats has quite rightly shifted the emphasis towards "redistribution of possibilities". The cultivation of human potential should as far as possible replace "after the event" redistribution.'[5]

Indeed, as Michael Young points out,[6] New Labour's policy is even less radical than Giddens', tending to ignore voluntary social exclusion at the top of society and focusing on compensatory programmes at the bottom. In addition, Labour appears to be deeply wedded to a protestant work ethic, seeing paid employment as the main vehicle of inclusion. The value of education is deemed to lie in its effect on the employability of the individual. Ruth Lister's critique emphasises that this limited approach is unlikely to produce the virtuous circle that Labour seeks. She writes:

> *Inclusion into the bottom rung of an unequal society in which the rich are able to exclude themselves from the common bonds of citizenship is a less inspiring vision. Current policy tends to equate social inclusion with paid work, supported by education. Paid work is important. But it does not necessarily spell genuine social inclusion for those trapped in dead-end jobs ... Moreover, the fetishism of paid work can serve to undervalue other forms of work such as community and voluntary work and unpaid care work in the home. So, while paid work and education represent important building blocks in the construction of an inclusive society, they should be seen as part of a wider architecture, infused with the principles of citizenship.[7]*

It is the neglect of economic equality that critics of Third Way politics see as a fundamental weakness. They would argue that the evils of persistent ill-health and under-achievement are not the product of social exclusion but the consequences of economic inequality.[8] Anne Phillips argues that the emphasis on political and civil equalities has masked the neglect of more profound and discriminatory material inequality.[9] Indeed, the Countryside Alliance's at least partial success in marshalling a whole range of rural discontents to a conservative cause has resulted from using just such egalitarian language. Their rhetoric about the 'urban jackboot' argues for an equal and, implicitly, a semi-independent devolved status for rural areas, thereby (ironically) seeking to sustain the power of the land-owning classes within the countryside.

That said, the concept of social exclusion can be highly pertinent. Graham Harvey, in his trenchant polemic on contemporary agricultural practices and subsidies, describes the current situation for rural communities:

> *Even in urban Britain in the 1990s, one-third of the population is described as 'predominantly rural' or 'significantly rural'. But because most of them are landless they have no control over their local environment, beyond complaining about mud in the road or the smell of pig slurry. They have no stake in the countryside; they are effectively excluded. They live on the periphery like temporary expatriates in some foreign land. It was not always so.[10]*

Thus Harvey links social exclusion to material inequality. In effect, he argues that social exclusion is the *result* of economic marginalisation rather than its *cause*. That marginalisation, he asserts, is the result of the concentration of the ownership of land and the consequent exclusion of the people. 'Exclusion – of small farmers, of the rural poor and of the public – lies at the heart of our national malaise.'[11] This critique is promoted by the small, but active, land rights campaign: 'The Land is Ours'.[12]

Harvey's radical interpretation points to an important dimension of rural inequality. What he graphically demonstrates is that the restructuring of just one key rural economic activity, agriculture, has had social consequences that a doctrine of individual responsibility can neither explain nor rectify. However, whether his analysis, so reminiscent of Henry George, is sufficient to explain all aspects of rural deprivation is questionable. Instead, rural social exclusion must be seen as a multi-faceted, dynamic process that both causes and consolidates inequalities. It is one that involves changes to the social, economic and demographic infrastructure. These changes have produced patterns of rural deprivation which are related to a number of factors: demographic (age and gender); economic (employment and services); and communal (through the marginalisation of communities). Rural social exclusion is a complex phenomenon.

Rural social exclusion

This linkage between socio-economic change and social exclusion requires an analysis of the pattern of that change. The most ubiquitous economic activity in rural areas would seem to be agriculture. It would appear to be the mainstay of the local economy. However, with the substantial re-structuring of post-war farming, it has ceased to be the main source of employment for local communities. Nationally, only 1.8 per cent of the workforce is employed in agriculture. In rural areas this rises to only 4.4 per cent.[13]

There are two clear trends. The first is that the number of holdings is falling and the average size of farms expanding. The encouragement of highly-mechanised, 'efficient' agriculture has been at the expense of smaller, more labour-intensive operations. The result is the second trend: falling agricultural employment. Harvey claims that a workforce that stood at around one million at the end of the war had, by 1994, fallen to 120,000, whilst the 1990s saw an annual 12 per cent reduction in jobs.[14] The Countryside Agency suggests that this is overstated. Their figures show that 417,400 people were employed in agriculture in 1997, but they do confirm an even sharper drop in employment. An estimated 60,500 jobs were lost between 1987 and 1997, 14 per cent of the workforce.[15]

These trends have been exacerbated by the introduction of set-aside as a solution to overproduction and the current farm crisis. The collapse of livestock prices has been spectacular. Yet this has remained hidden from general view, as the reductions have not been passed on to consumers. The National Farmer's

Union claims that between 1997 and 1999 farm incomes fell by 75 per cent to an average of £8,000.[16] The causes of this decline are complex and long-term. However, the process was accelerated by the BSE crisis.[17] Quite clearly this has affected public confidence in the farming industry and has lessened sympathy for the plight of agriculture in an urbanised country, regardless of the crisis having political as much as agricultural origins.

The government's initial response was slow. Its speculation about a farmers' redundancy scheme[18] – which, if implemented, would further weaken agriculture as a source of employment and economic viability for local communities – could hardly be described as adequate. However, the escalating crisis forced a response. In a poorly-received speech to the National Farmer's Union[19] Tony Blair held out the promise of cash but only if 'tied to long-term change and reform.'[20] That change amounted to little more than further intensification and diversification. The nod towards organic farming was swamped by the message on market efficiency. The following day the Prime Minister toured rural areas to give an upbeat message on their economic health. This peculiar tactic of telling people that they are doing well despite their day-to-day experience is much beloved by the political class. This time it betrayed the lack of analysis at the heart of government thinking.

The government's response to the 2001 Foot and Mouth epidemic was similarly confused. Lord Haskins, the Chairman of Northern Foods, was appointed as Rural Recovery Co-ordinator in August 2001. An outspoken critic of organic production and small farms, he courted controversy immediately with his claim that half of British farms would disappear in the next twenty years. This prompted comments that a cull of animals was to be followed by a cull of farmers. Despite this spin, the consequent published report[21] was bland and brief.

This response only confirms the uncoupling of the rural economy from agriculture. Diversification into leisure and the ubiquitous 'e-business' confirms that the mainstay of employment has to continue to be in light industry and services. Yet these too have suffered as a result of the 'rationalisations' of the 1980s and 1990s. Rural areas have little competitive advantage. Their infrastructure is worse and transport costs higher, offsetting the low wages. Suppliers of goods and services to agriculture, who do have a local market, have felt the impact of the agricultural crisis. Rural communities also form a dispersed, minority market of marginal commercial viability. Adult educators have long been aware of the difficulty of enrolling sustainable groups.

As a result, the replacement of a service ethos with a commercial one, in both the public and private sector, has led to the loss of facilities for smaller communities. Public services, never comparable with those of urban areas but scarcely meeting rural needs, are under increasing pressure. Local authority services are hit by the discrimination against rural areas in assessing the Standard Spending Assessment (SSA). On average, the SSA for metropolitan districts (excluding London) in 1997–8 was £717 per person. The SSA for the mostly rural shire counties was £670 per person.[22] This produces both reductions in employment opportunities and increasing costs and inconvenience.

This also interacts with the private sector. Rural post offices, a hybrid of public and private, have been threatened by the decision to pay benefits through credit transfer to bank accounts. The campaign to save them has been sustained by unlikely institutions such as the Women's Institute (WI). This no doubt contributed to Tony Blair's unpleasant experience at the WI annual conference in June 2000. But one of the most significant recent factors has been the growing concentration of ownership in the private sector. The decline in independent traders and the rise in large chains have led to the loss of facilities; the spate of bank branch closures in early 2000 being just one example. The resulting remoteness of decision-making from communities renders protest ineffective. This can have a profound effect on local communities. For example, the drop in the number of rural dispensing chemists shows how the loss of a commercial outlet can literally become a charge on some of the most vulnerable members of the community, the sick and the old.[23]

The State of the Countryside report lists an alarming lack of local amenities.[24] In 1997:

- 42 per cent of rural parishes had no shop
- 70 per cent did not have a general store
- 43 per cent had no post office
- 28 per cent had no village hall or community centre
- 75 per cent had no daily bus service
- 49 per cent had no school (for any age)
- 29 per cent had no pub
- 83 per cent had no GP based in the parish.

The advent of the National Lottery saw a spate of village hall development and renovation but, with changes to the Lottery's Community Fund, even this boost to rural amenities appears to have ceased. Action with Communities in Rural England (ACRE) reported that:

ACRE's work with Village Halls Advisers, based in Rural Community Councils, demonstrate that substantially less funding is available for capital improvements for village halls from April 2002. There is now a major funding gap of around £50m with apparent current financial resources targeted towards top-down, geographically or priority-led bids.[25]

The combination of service depletion, the size of the rural market and lower local government spending impacts on employment prospects in the local economy. It has meant an extraordinary dependence on small businesses and a slightly greater proportion of part-time jobs. In 1998 in Rural Development Areas, 91.4 per cent of all VAT registered enterprises had fewer than 10 employees whilst 26.4 per cent of working people were in part-time employment, compared to 25.1 per cent in England as a whole.[26] In line with national trends, the growth in part-time work is part of a feminisation of the workforce. Male full-time jobs are being lost. This creates pockets of relative deprivation for those employed in the local economy. Not only is part-time work lower paid and insecure, there are sharp gender differentials in earnings.

In North Yorkshire in the late 1990s, for example, household disposable income per head of population was 8.6 per cent above the national average and headline unemployment well below it.[27] However, North Yorkshire Training and Enterprise Council noted that 'the number of full-time employees as a percentage of all employees has fallen from 66.7 per cent to 51.8 per cent in 1997. This is expected to fall further over the next six years as the number of part-time and temporary jobs increases.'[28] In 1995, North Yorkshire's average male manual earnings were £279 and non-manual earning were £385. The female equivalents were £169 and £246 respectively.[29] It is hard to find evidence of post-feminism in rural areas whilst this gender disadvantage exacerbates the decline in earning power of parts of the community.

Part-time working is compounded by seasonal disadvantage. The long-term trend of rural Britain, changing from being a location for production to a venue for leisure consumption, can only be exacerbated by the response to the farm crisis. Tourism has become one of the cornerstones of the rural service economy. However, much of it is seasonal by its very nature. 'The season' becomes a source of casual employment, only for workers to be jettisoned onto benefits for the winter. In the north of the country the season can be painfully short.

This pattern of disadvantage would suggest that rural areas are sunk in poverty, but this is manifestly untrue. Every indicator points the other way. Unemployment is lower than the national average with employment growth in some sectors; the housing stock is better maintained; the property market is buoyant; educational attainment is higher; whilst the population is growing. Of course, average figures will always mask the existence of localised deprivation. However, in rural areas they point to a process of demographic change which itself is part of the development of social exclusion.

Deprivation and the countryside

The discussion of rural deprivation involves three distinct aspects. The first is the necessity of distinguishing between central and peripheral rural areas. The further away from the metropolitan centres of the country, the more widespread is the overall pattern of deprivation. Thus Cornwall is the least prosperous county in England. It has the lowest level of gross domestic product per head of population and, in the late 1990s, an average weekly wage was £88 below the national average.[30] The second is the dispersed nature of deprivation. Unlike urban areas it is hard to undertake a postcode analysis of poverty. This is especially so since the sale of council houses has meant that those with low incomes are housed in the private rented sector.[31] Thus deprivation is hidden amongst affluent communities and concealed by gender bias in policy making.

The third aspect emphasises a process by which the poor and rurally-born are gradually being marginalised from both the social and economic centre of rural life. This process is most properly named social exclusion.

A key to understanding rural social exclusion is to realise that quantitative measures of economic hardship and service depletion are not the only aspect of rural deprivation. Social exclusion is a qualitative experience as well. Not only does the dispersal of deprivation result in the isolation of the individual within a prosperous community but the experience also, as Scott emphasises, involves a sense of loss of something valued.[31] That loss is not merely of services but of a sense of community and identity. This has been accelerated by the demographic changes in rural areas.

The population of rural England is growing but ageing. It is mainly the result of in-migration of older people and out-migration of the young. Crucially, this is linked to changes in urban Britain. The major urban centres are losing population and this is an exodus of the affluent. This may cause concern to urban planners but its impact on rural society is no less profound.

The desire to live in the countryside is a product of deep cultural impulses. The romanticisation of rural life has been a constant in the myth of Englishness, despite (or because of?) the urban nature of the nation. The acquisitiveness of Thatcherite and post-Thatcherite culture has led to the commodification of lifestyles. At a price, the affluent can buy their urban loft or their rural idyll. Those who choose the countryside have a vision that is shaped by a romanticism rather than any concept of the reality of a working community and landscape. They pay large sums for their second homes or commuter lifestyles. They do not see their purchase as conditional. The realities of a working rural population form no part of their dream.

The most important economic effect is that there are *two* economies in the countryside. There is the urban economy, which provides the income of commuters and second homeowners and the pensions of the retired. Secondly, there is a local economy to which the increasingly immobile rural poor are tied. Thus the positive statistics are the result of the effects of the first and mask the consequences of the second. There is little evidence of 'trickle down' from one to the other. Instead what emerges is a pattern of dominance by the affluent over the local.

Whether consciously or unconsciously, incomers can, if they wish to participate, dominate local services,[33] decision-making bodies and social institutions. By doing so they set an agenda which suits their needs. Alternatively, they can absent themselves from the community, using their spending power in urban areas. The local economy is starved of custom, local services collapse, whilst the housing market suffers gross distortion. House prices become linked to the urban middle-class property market rather than the low-wage rural economy. It is estimated that two thirds of all households cannot afford to buy an appropriately-sized home.[34] Unsurprisingly homelessness is growing faster in rural areas than in urban ones.

The economic effects are but one aspect of this process. Certainly, it leads to the physical dispossession of local people. They are unable to live in the villages that had been the homes of their families. However, it also creates social marginalisation as the affluent reshape the community according to their own needs and perceptions. Whether deliberately or not, the culture of the new arrivals is one of exclusion, redefining rural people and rural life.[35] It would not be much of an overstatement to compare locally-born populations with indigenous peoples displaced by colonial settlers the world over. It is apposite that some radical Scottish nationalists colloquially refer to English migrants as 'white settlers'.

It is arguable that this process of marginalisation is one of the most debilitating aspects of rural life for deprived communities. Displacement and loss of esteem lead to low educational attainment and patterns of local employment that sees locals working in the lowest-paid sectors. Professional, well-paid work is often the province of the incomer. In this way social exclusion is created through a process of social change, but it has different effects on different sections of the community.

One of the most marginalised groups in rural society is the young. This marginalisation can embrace the children of incomers as much as the locally born, although the former group often have greater access to economic, educational and cultural resources that can be used as a means of escape. Already susceptible to unemployment and low pay, and discriminated against by minimum-wage legislation and the withdrawal of benefits, young people face a dearth of facilities and hostility from those seeking peace and quiet. School league tables also tend to encourage exclusion of disruptive young people, closing avenues of opportunities. As Michael Simmons comments:

> *Boredom and being misunderstood are the key issues for young people in rural areas. For them more than most, 'peace and quiet' can only mean 'nothing going on', while 'unhurried lifestyle' suggests a sub existence which is slow and unexciting. What some may seize upon as 'traditional rural values' can be the vehicle for expressing disapproval of young people's unacceptable activities and tastes, their point of view and their aspirations.[36]*

As a result, rural communities experience phenomena more closely associated with urban areas. Simmons again:

> *It soon becomes apparent that 19-year-olds who have been unemployed since they left school three years earlier, do not make the best mentors for bored adolescents, especially the under-educated. A willingness at least to experiment with alcohol, window cleaning fluid, glue or hard drugs, or to dabble in the world of crime, becomes understandable. The British National Party has been known to trawl the country areas for new recruits.[37]*

A recent survey suggests that whilst 19.2 per cent of 14–15-year-old boys and 16.6 per cent of girls in cities had experimented with illegal drugs, 27.4 per cent *of both boys and girls* in rural areas had experience of drug taking.[38] The issue of gender is also central to the understanding of rural deprivation. The responsibility for family budgets rests mainly on women, whilst they are increasingly members of a low-paid, part-time workforce. Rural single parents face the same problem of low income as urban ones, hardly helped by Labour's astonishing decision to cut benefits. However, they do so in a context of minimal services and debilitating social isolation. One project found that 35 per cent of rural single parents were in weekly contact with five people or less. Unsurprisingly, loneliness and coping with their own emotional needs were seen to be the major problems faced.[39]

Those unable to participate in the workforce face even greater hardship. The whole thrust of Labour's policy on social exclusion has been towards moving people into work. People dependent on benefits have faced hard times. Those on disability benefits, for example, not only face new restrictions on eligibility but have also undergone the Benefit Integrity Project. Rural people are especially vulnerable as the effect of isolation and service depletion is in itself disabling. The effect of disability is magnified by rural conditions. Thus a medical assessment alone is inadequate for assessing benefit eligibility as it ignores the social context in which the person has to operate. The elderly, for long the mainstay of liberal adult education, are more likely to be reliant on the state pension if they are locally born and have earned their living in the rural economy. The difficulties the Labour Party faced with a conference defeat in 2000 over the failure to reverse the Conservative's earlier uncoupling of pensions from average earnings, showed the growth of unease over increasing inequalities. In rural areas this is manifested by the problems faced by local pensioners in participating in an economic and social system where the cost base is shaped by those with access to private pensions or the proceeds of property sales. This serves to aggravate social and economic polarisation.

The challenge for lifelong learning

Faced with this degree of disadvantage buried in an affluent society, it is a daunting task for lifelong learning to be 'the key to social cohesion'. Profound social and economic change cannot be generated through adult education in village halls. Although lifelong learning needs to develop a sense of mission to respond to rural needs, it would be wrong to assert that it is the solution to rural disadvantage, despite New Labour's ideology. The record of compensatory programmes is hardly encouraging – whilst for the elderly and isolated, for example, learning may be a social salvation but it represents a cost rather than a method of enhancing income. However, programmes can be tailored to address aspects of social exclusion, and should be specifically targeted. The Woodrow Report has argued convincingly that, without targeting, new opportunities are monopolised by the advantaged to the exclusion of the disadvantaged.[40] To operate effectively it has to reflect the differential impact of social change on generations of potential learners. It also means justifying provision in terms of the social function that it performs. CE has often played a key role in community care but has been unwilling to acknowledge the fact.

Lifelong learning can begin to address skills deficits and the lack of a learning infrastructure for rural communities. Community development programmes can promote social reintegration. But it cannot do so in a vacuum. It requires institutional and governmental commitment to resourcing a provision that will never generate high numbers of participants. It needs the development of appropriate delivery methodologies. But, above all, it needs the political realisation that the elimination of social exclusion requires a commitment to social justice. Whether New Labour will grasp this remains to be seen.

Notes

1. *The Guardian*, 9, 10 & 11 March 1998.
2. *The Observer*, 22 February 1998.
3. See the Countryside Alliance website at http://www.countryside-alliance.org for details.
4. Giddens, A. (1998). *The Third Way: The Renewal of Social Democracy*. Polity Press; pp. 102–3.
5. *Ibid.*, p. 101.
6. Young, M. (1999). Some reflections: beyond The Third Way. In Hayton, A. ed. *Tackling Disaffection and Social Exclusion: Education Perspective and Policies*. Kogan Page; p. 213.
7. Lister, R. (1999). First steps to a fairer society. *The Guardian*, June 9.
8. See Wilkinson, R. (1996). *Unhealthy Societies: The Afflictions of Inequality*. Routledge.
9. Phillips, A. (1999). *Which Equalities Matter?* Polity Press.
10. Harvey, G. (1998). *The Killing of the Countryside*. Vintage; p. 156.
11. *Ibid.*, p.165.
12. For full details and an interesting archive of materials see The Land is Ours website at http://www.enviroweb.org/tlio.
13. The Countryside Agency (1999). *Rural Economic Bulletin 2*. Cheltenham.
14. Harvey, *op. cit.*, pp. 72–73.
15. The Countryside Agency (1999). *The State of the Countryside*. Cheltenham; p. 20.
16. *The Guardian*, 1 September 1999.
17. The Foot and Mouth epidemic is likely to have a similar reinforcing impact [ed].
18. *The Guardian*, 27 August 1999.
19. Except in The Archers on BBC Radio 4 where it inspired some incredibly stilted dialogue.
20 *The Guardian*, 2 February 2000.
21. Haskins, C. *Rural Recovery after Foot and Mouth Disease*. Department for Environment, Food and Rural Affairs, 2 October 2001. http://www.defra.gov.uk/footandmouth/rural/taskforce/Haskins.PDF

22. The Countryside Agency (1999). *The State of the Countryside*; p. 28.

23. Scott, D., Shenton, S. and Healey, B. (1991). *Hidden Deprivation in the Countryside, Local Studies in the Peak National Park*. Peak Park Trust.

24. The Countryside Agency (1999). *The State of the Countryside*; p. 26.

25. Action with Communities in Rural England (2002). *The Status of Funding for Village Halls. A Regional and National Perspective. Executive Summary*. http://www.acre.org.uk/Village_hall_funding_SUMMARY_document.htm

26. *Ibid.*, p. 15.

27. North Yorkshire Training and Enterprise Council (1999). *Labour Market Review*.

28. North Yorkshire Training and Enterprise Council (1998). *Corporate Plan 1998-2001*.

29. Campbell, M., Foy, S. and Walton, F. (1996). *Rural Issues in Yorkshire and Humberside*. Policy Research Institute.

30. The Countryside Agency (1999). *The State of the Countryside*; pp. 16–17.

31. 91,000 rural homes were lost from the social rented sector between 1995 and 1990. The Countryside Agency (1999). *The State of the Countryside*; p. 25.

32. Scott, *op. cit.*, p. 20.

33. At least one survey asserts that this is as true of continuing education as any other service. See Lowerson, J. and Thomson, A. eds. (1994). *Out of Sight, Out of Mind: Barriers to Participation in Rural Adult Education*. Centre for Continuing Education, the University of Sussex. The author's own experience would reinforce this perception.

34. The Countryside Agency (1999). *The State of the Countryside*; p. 25.

35. See Sibley, D. (1995). *Geographies of Exclusion: Society and Difference in the West*. Routledge.

36. Simmons, M. (1997). *Landscapes of Poverty: Aspects of Rural England in the Late 1990s*. Lemos and Crane; p. 67.

37. *Ibid.*, p. 69.

38. *The Guardian*, 11 March 1998.

39. Joseph Rowntree Foundation (1996). Evaluation of a self-help support project for rural lone parents. *Social Policy Research 108*.

40. Woodrow, M. *et al.* (1998). *From Elitism to Inclusion: Good Practice in Widening Access to Higher Education*. CVCP.

4

Rural adult education in Britain: a historical survey

William R. Jones

Introduction

The spectator gazed on and on till the windows and vanes lost their shine, going out almost suddenly like extinguished candles. The vague city became veiled in mist ... 'It is a city of light,' he said to himself. 'The tree of knowledge grows there,' he added a few steps further on.

Thomas Hardy, Jude the Obscure

Thus the eponymous hero of *Jude the Obscure* sees a distant prospect of educational opportunity, as he gazes over the miles to Christminster (Oxford) from the rural isolation of the Berkshire Ridgeway. Nearby is his home village of Marygreen, rapidly becoming depopulated by the exodus to the towns and, at the opening of the novel, losing its only schoolmaster. Literature can provide us with telling examples of the prehistory of organised provision in rural areas and *Jude* is an oft-cited fictional text in the history of adult education.

Although the majority of the population lived in the country, the eighteenth-century beginnings of adult education in a recognisable form evolved in the towns. The Sunday schools, mechanics' institutes and other early forms of organised provision were set up in cities and urban manufacturing communities, particularly those which had grown rapidly since the Industrial Revolution. Institutions such as the Working Men's Colleges and Institutes were well established by the mid-nineteenth century, by which time debate had begun on the nature and control of the curriculum.

By contrast, there was very little (and mostly *ad hoc*) provision for learning, either for children or adults, in rural communities. A member of a cottage family in an agricultural village had only such opportunity as was offered by chance. A prime example was Stephen Duck, the 'thresher poet' of the eighteenth century. Duck was born in 1705 in the village of Charlton in Wiltshire. Brought up to farm labour, he was determined on self-improvement through reading, thinking and working at arithmetic. By working extra hours, he was able to buy a few books which he studied by night. His intellectual promise and determination drew the attention of local gentry who provided him with books and helped his learning. One of his patrons was Joseph Spence, Professor of Poetry at Oxford. Spence later wrote: 'Considering the difficulties ... the inclination for Knowledge must have been very strong in him.'

Duck developed an aptitude for verse and wrote *The Thresher's Labour*, a long poem uniquely descriptive of the working year of the farm labourer. His reputation spread and his benefactors obtained an introduction to the Queen who was sufficiently impressed by this earnest countryman to employ Duck as her librarian at Kew. The 'Thresher' became a literary nine-days' wonder, even to the extent of being considered for the Laureateship. Unfortunately this rapid elevation not only destroyed his individuality as a poet but also his mind. In 1756 he took his own life.

A similar case is that of Mary Collier (1688–1762).[1] Born in Sussex, she worked all her life both as a fieldwoman and domestic servant. She also showed great determination as a learner, and achieved a measure of fame with the publication of her poems. These included a riposte to Duck entitled *The Woman's Labour*, in which she describes the travails of the working woman as greater than those of the labouring man. In the preface she movingly describes her hard-won learning, the struggles to acquire books and to find time for reading and self-improvement alongside a 12-hour working day: 'I was taught to read when very Young, and took great delight in it; but my Mother dying, I lost my education, never being put to School. My Recreation was reading, I bought and borrow'd many Books.'[2] As a young woman, she lived with her father 'who before his death was long sickly and infirm. After his Death being left alone, I came to Petersfield where my chief employment was, Washing, Brewing and such labour, still devoting what leisure time I had to Books.'

There are other examples of men and women from rural origins who struggled to achieve a measure of learning and modest reputations as writers. James Hogg (1770–1835), the 'Ettrick Shepherd', is a well-known Scottish example.[3] These stories exemplify the lack of anything beyond luck or sheer doggedness to assist rural learners who wanted to better themselves in the eighteenth century. It also indicates Establishment attitudes to such learning opportunity – at best paternalistic benevolence, at worst the parading of these 'discoveries' as prodigies in much the same way as South Sea Islanders were put on public view in London. Fame soon abandoned Mary Collier to a garret in Petersfield, where she died in poverty.

There was a tradition of schooling for rural communities, but it was very haphazard and inadequate and based in village schools of very varying capacity and quality. Organised education developed in the seventeenth and eighteenth centuries. The establishment of the Society for the Propagation of Christian Knowledge in 1699 led to a wide network of charity schools. Later, the dissenting movement, especially the Wesleyan Methodist societies, added their distinctive provision of Sunday schools for children and adults alike. In Wales and Scotland the provision generally lagged behind England, owing to the more scattered population and the isolation of communities; but, again, there was a tradition of education which could be traced back, in some cases, to the Middle Ages and the role of the bards as popular teachers and transmitters of history and culture.

Some enlightened innovations also took place. Griffith Jones, rector of Llandowror in Carmarthenshire, set his face against the existing elementary schools, which taught in English and charged fees, and set up his successful experiment of free schools. These taught the most basic subjects – literacy and catechism – in Welsh, through circulating schools which moved on regularly. His annual report for 1743–4 describes the schools, which by the late 1730s had become a flourishing movement:

> *No pompous preparation or costly buildings … but a Church or Chapel, or untenanted house … all sorts that desire it are to be kindly and freely taught for Three Months … not only to teach the Poor to Read, but to instruct them daily … in the Principles and Duties of religion.*[4]

Students ranged in age from six to 70 years. It is said that Jones developed his idea from the Scottish charity schools, set up by the Scottish equivalent of the SPCK and which numbered over 300 by the end of the eighteenth century. In the very large rural parishes of the Highlands these 'ambulatory' schools moved on to new communities after a few months in each:

> *With the Bible in one hand and the three R's in the other the schoolmaster penetrated to the most remote and backward parts, teaching and preaching as he went, and as in Wales, he left behind him men and women who could read the Bible and could, moreover, teach others to read it too.*[5]

This, then, was the state of affairs up to about 1870. Two events then occurred which directly impacted on educational opportunity and provision in rural areas for both children and adults. These were, respectively, the Education Act of 1870, and the development of the university extension movement to rural communities.

The 1870 Education Act

The 1870 Act had a profound effect in general, but for our present purposes it transformed the provision of education in rural areas. In contrast to previous provision, which was sporadic even in the best-served areas, the new legislation (with its introduction of the concept of universal schooling for children up to the age of thirteen) for the first time forced the issue of implementing educational entitlement in remote rural areas with small or scattered populations.[6] Subsequent modifications to the regulations increased the responsibility on both parents and local authorities to ensure attendance by children from remote locations; for example, the introduction of transport for pupils from 1899. Another significant change was the introduction of minimum acceptable standards for buildings, a consequence of which was a period of school building by the new education authorities.

It could be argued that this concept articulated for the first time the central dilemma of rural education, and especially education beyond primary school: the problem of how to achieve a viable critical mass of learners in a dispersed population without forcing them to migrate from country to town. Often the solution results in a tendency to centralise education at a distance, necessitating travel from rural communities to centres of population. This tendency, whilst acknowledged as having some benefits for learners, was recognised as early as 1907 as contributing to 'the movement against which so much effort ... is devoted, the continuous replenishment of the towns at the expense of the country and the draining of the country of some of the best elements in its life.'[7]

University extension and rural areas

The university extension movement began in 1868 with the lecture tours of James Stuart of Cambridge for the working populations of northern manufacturing cities. The movement also reached some rural areas where there were concentrations of population, such as mining communities. In the Northumberland mining villages, there was a vigorous extension programme drawing on the pioneering work of Cambridge – and especially that of James Stuart, who came to the mining community of Backworth in 1881 at the invitation of the newly-formed Students' Association to lecture on mathematics. Other subjects covered were physiology, English literature and ancient Greek comedy, the latter proving a difficult topic for many students. The thirst for learning in these Northumberland pit villages was intense, with miners buying academic books and making great efforts to attend the lectures. R.D. Roberts, in *Eighteen Years in University Extension*, gives an instance of this:

> Two pitmen brothers, living in a village five miles from one of the centres, were able to get in to the lectures by train, but the return service was inconvenient and they were compelled to walk home. This they did weekly for three months, on dark nights, over wretchedly bad roads and in all kinds of weather. On one occasion they returned in a severe storm, when the roads were so flooded that they lost their way and got up to their waists in water. It is not surprising to find that they distinguished themselves in the examination and eventually succeeded in making their own village a lecture-centre.[8]

This was seen as a model for a further stage of university extension from towns to villages. As Roberts put it: 'Here we see the earliest beginnings of a subsidiary system suited to the needs of villages and rural districts.'[9] The approach was extended to other parts of the country. In 1889 a local committee organised Cambridge extension lectures in two Surrey villages. The lectures were fortnightly, with the intervening weeks taught by a student. In Yorkshire the pattern was a single lecture in the village, 'inciting those more eager for knowledge to go to Barnsley for the regular course.'[10]

It is noteworthy that even at this early date the necessity of local rather than visiting tutors to undertake some of the teaching was recognised. In the Northumberland pit villages, pressure for such appointments began in the early

1880s, partly for practical reasons of providing effective tuition at such a distance from Cambridge, but also on account of cost. At the 1890 Cambridge Extension Conference, a speaker advocated 'a plan whereby student lecturers, trained at University extension centres, who have given evidence of their capacity, should go into the villages to hold small classes, and so leaven the whole lump of rural life.'[11] The same speaker expressed the needs of the rural communities with evangelical fervour:

> If the University desires to do a thoroughly good work ... it cannot do better than to enlighten the intellectual darkness in rural districts. Anything more utterly monotonous or miserable to persons of either sex with intellectual tastes than the ordinary life of country villages I cannot conceive.[12]

These dismal conclusions are borne out by other writers. A 1907 survey found that the various agencies of further education, whatever their success in the cities, were 'a pretty general failure ... in most rural districts in England. The young people grow up in an atmosphere which, as a rule, nips educational ambitions in the bud.'[13] In Wales and Scotland the picture was equally unsatisfactory; apart from Sunday schools, there was very little organised provision in Wales, while in Scotland, it was claimed, even the Sunday schools were little regarded.

In the early years of the twentieth century, therefore, there was little in the way of organised rural adult education to match the comparatively well-developed urban provision. University extension had reached some communities, and the issue of delivering universal schooling to scattered and small villages had been brought to the fore by the Education Act and subsequent legislation.

The First World War

At the outbreak of the First World War the situation was therefore that the educational needs of village communities were recognised, but without local infrastructure the only provision for continuing education had to be in the larger centres. This tended to add to the drain of the more able to the towns. The Workers' Educational Association (WEA) had started to gain a foothold in rural areas, especially in the south, but this was placed in serious jeopardy by the war. The following is from the WEA's 1918 *Yearbook*:

> The rural work of the Association has suffered more than any other activity through the difficulties caused by the war. In several districts, where the movement was taking root in small villages, the obstacles caused by increased railway fares and disorganisation of trains have made it almost impossible to carry on the work ... but there is good ground for the belief that when the opportunity arrives the work in villages will grow rapidly; this appears to be especially so in the Eastern, South-Eastern and Western Districts. A special committee of the central Council is at present inquiring into the whole subject.[14]

The '1919 Report'

The *Yearbook* makes various references to the end of the war and the reconstruction of educational provision and infrastructure that would be required. The Reconstruction Committee was already in existence by 1917, in which year it commissioned a special report on adult education. *The Final Report of the Adult Education Committee of the Ministry of Reconstruction,*[15] now popularly known as the '1919 Report', set out recommendations which brought into being the structure and financial principles of modern adult education. Appendix 1: 'A Survey of Adult Education' has a special section on 'Adult Education in Rural Districts' which draws attention both to the general lack of organised rural provision and to the absence of the community-based organisations that underpin it.

An Interim Report on Industrial and Social Conditions in Relation to Adult Education contains a section on 'The Rural Problem'.[16] This makes depressing reading, at least insofar as it describes England; Wales and Scotland were separated out for praise for the educational and cultural standards in village life. However English rural life was seen as uncompromisingly hostile to educational development. Over one million agricultural workers lived in sub-standard housing and lacked security of tenure. Work was hard and sometimes uncertain:

> The rural worker has not only the ever-present worry of how to subsist, he has often the dread of unemployment in long spells of wet weather. The result only too often is general depression and lack of interest ... Those beyond 25 years of age were usually so absorbed in making both ends meet that they had little inclination to take part in work of an educational character. Villagers below that age did not seem to regard village life as a permanency.[17]

The young people of the village tended to head for the town for recreation, '... made possible by the advent of the cheap cycle. They never [the report continues] learn to realise themselves as an essential part of their little village community'.[18] In addition, to this inhospitable climate for enhanced rural educational opportunity, there was opposition from the village Establishment:

> The view that education is superfluous for hewers of wood and drawers of water has not yet been finally discredited even in the towns; in the country it still persists and manifests itself in an opposition to non-vocational education, which is regarded not merely as unnecessary, but as dangerous to the stability of rural society.[19]

A number of examples are cited: 'In the majority of cases where we have started rural study groups, the principal farmer in the neighbourhood has attempted to upset it in his village by coming down and protesting in person,' writes a local rural organiser from the south; while the local WEA Secretary in a Wiltshire village adds:

> Here we had a quite decent parish room, but unfortunately its management was largely in the hands of several very narrow-minded and unprogressive people ... Through their influence the WEA was debarred from all further use of the room, because a perfectly impartial survey of village life from early times was given in which the Enclosures and the work of Joseph Arch were referred to.[20]

Indeed one respondent from the West Country was of the view that 'the public house is the only place where men can meet ... as to women, it is very rare to find a suitable meeting-place.'[21]

The main report makes a number of specific recommendations, based on the premise that rural educational activity will only follow a general restoration of the social and economic well-being of rural society:

> *The full development of adult education is impossible apart from the realisation of a comprehensive rural programme. ... The rural problem, from whatever point of view it is regarded – economic, social or political – is essentially a problem of re-creating the rural community, of developing new social traditions and a new culture. The great need is for a living nucleus of communal activity in the village ... We conceive the nucleus to be a village institute, under full public control.[22]*

The report discusses at length the educational activities that might be appropriate for the village institute. These range from practical courses on, for example, horticulture and husbandry (which would relate to the vocational curriculum of the county agricultural colleges) to non-vocational and recreational topics.

Many villages were found to have existing halls and institutes that had fallen into near-dereliction. The report is adamant that capital expenditure is an overwhelming requirement, and makes the recommendation for public funding to cover up to 90 per cent of the building cost. Other recommendations address the issue of devolving the existing educational facilities to village level; for instance, library stock to circulate locally, and – very important for the structure of adult education providers – 'the development of a system of resident tutors and the decentralisation of university extra-mural education ... we regard the gradual establishment of resident tutors and lecturers in rural areas as a necessary part of ... rural education.'[23]

At last, therefore, a comprehensive system of provision for rural communities was recognised as essential and given a structure that, in due course, was largely implemented. But these improvements did not come rapidly; nor was the enthusiasm of the report for non-vocational adult education matched by popular demand. In 1924 a leading article in the *Times Educational Supplement* complained that:

> *The rural problem is one that successive governments have ignored in despair ... the lack of facilities for ... continued education is a disgrace to a highly organised community. All the necessary things can be done. What we wish to emphasise is that they are not being done, and they do not seem likely to be done.[24]*

The 1922 Report

Despite concern about the speed of action, there was a very considerable drive at policy level for the development of rural adult education in the 1920s. A large part of this impetus derived from the recent experience of the necessity of the country being self-sufficient in wartime:

> *But the work of the Ministry of Agriculture ... the Universities and the Agricultural colleges will come to little unless it is accompanied by a higher standard of education ... which will prevent the drift of the most intelligent men to the towns. It must not be forgotten that agriculture ... is yet our largest industry, on which in the last resort the security of the nation depends. In this as in other matters the education of the nation is its surest defence.*

This quote is from *The Development of Adult Education in Rural Areas* (1922)[25] – the third of the series of reports by the Adult Education Committee of the Board of Education published throughout the 1920s on key areas of the adult education agenda. This report is one of the very few documents to deal exclusively and at length with rural provision, and to address its peculiarities. It is the first to offer a definition of 'rural' for this purpose: 'those areas which are definitely dependent on agricultural interests, and, owing to distance or deficiency of transport, are little influenced by urban life.'[26]

As ever, the need is stressed for structures on which adult education can be grafted. There is praise for the 'great progress' of trade unions, and for the Women's Institute (WI). This movement, which began in Canada, was introduced here before the First World War, and during the war became important 'to assist in the production of food.' In the search for a structure for rural development, both unions and the WI are seen as having potential 'to facilitate the provision of adult education.' The WI responded to the challenge and by 1922 the Central Executive had set up a special Education Committee. Other structures mentioned include Village Clubs and the Oxford Rural Community Committee, which is especially identified as a model for linking villages in a county federation.[27]

The problems for the rural adult educator were listed in the report, and show strong similarities with those encountered today. They included low population density; high cost per student; transport difficulties; inadequate supply of tutors; 'diffidence' of countrymen to education; and with all these factors in a social context of isolation from the outside world.[28] But, again, the absence of infrastructure was highlighted. Even where problems were overcome, the lack of suitable premises could lead to failure. Often only the local primary school was available, with all its attendant inadequacies: 'It is generally necessary to sit on forms admirably adapted to infants but painful to their parents.'[29]

Nonetheless, by 1922 some progress was reported. Evidence was collected from both the WEA and the Local Education Authorities (LEAs) that revealed patchy successes. In Yorkshire, for example, the WEA District Secretary commented: 'The success which has attended the work has been considerable. Certainly for effort expended, the response has been infinitely greater than is usually obtained in the urban areas,'[30] while some LEAs were reported to be funding university and WEA initiatives. Another organisational scheme with adult educational potential was that of public libraries; by 1922 there were 22 Rural Library Schemes funded by the Carnegie Trust.[31]

But the overall picture in 1922 was, at best, one of sporadic success. There was no development of comprehensive adult education for rural areas. The WEA remained essentially an urban organisation, lacking the resource to fund the relatively expensive rural classes, and the LEAs were mostly unwilling to provide funding.[32] Solutions were proposed by all parties. The following is the collective view of the WEA District Secretaries:

> *The development of the rural areas requires 'peripatetic tutors' who will do more than lecture once weekly at a given place. The work can best be performed by having a full-time tutor for a given area, a collection of parishes, who can see to the organising side of class work as well as to the academic side.[33]*

The report concluded that 'schemes of rural education can secure immediate and notable success.'[34] The success of this would depend in particular on the establishment of Rural Community Councils; on a democratic management to 'encourage initiative and co-operation'; on the recruitment of a number of local full-time teaching staff; and on the building of village halls to accommodate classes. The curriculum was to be liberal as well as practical and vocational, and particular emphasis was given to the educational value of drama.

Village colleges

It was in this climate of a pressing need for co-ordinated action that Henry Morris, Director of Education for Cambridgeshire from 1922 to 1954, formed his concept of the village college. Often cited as a model for rural provision, the village college movement grew from Morris's high social and educational aims, which he articulated in 1924:

> *The time is ripe for a great constructive step forward in the rural problem. The work of re-establishing the life and welfare of the countryside is admitted to be really urgent … it is necessary that the problem of the reconstruction of the village should be dealt with in good time. There are certain economic aspects of rural welfare that can only be dealt with by governments; but all the other aspects of rural welfare are such as can be dealt with by education (in its widest sense) and by rebuilding the social life of the countryside.*

> *We must shift the centre of gravity of education from childhood to youth and maturity … In mediaeval Europe a common organisation was made possible by a system of common values and beliefs. In our time that element of unity in the life of society will be attained by the organisation of communities round their educational institutions … every local community will become an educational society.*

> *It would be a visible demonstration in stone of the continuity and never-ceasingness of education. There would be no 'leaving school' – the child would enter at three and leave the college only in extreme old age.*

> *The village college will be the seat and guardian of humane public traditions in the countryside. The training ground of a rural democracy realising its social and political duties.[35]*

The village colleges were designed to re-establish a vigorous rural community culture, and to counter the drift from country to town by establishing a college strategically positioned for the surrounding villages. The first was opened in 1930, six years after Morris's initial proposals, and four were in operation by the outbreak of the Second World War. These were founded on the vision and pragmatism of a determined individual who intended that they should be 'a new institution for the countryside ... that will touch every side of the life of the inhabitants ... conferring significance on their way of life.'[36] The vision would in due course spread to other counties: Devon, Somerset, Nottingham and Leicestershire – the latter's community colleges being directly inspired by the Cambridgeshire experiment.

As the 1920s progressed, many of the ideas and recommendations of the various policy initiatives began to bear fruit. The series of reports from the Adult Education Committee continued – the sixth, for example, being on *The Drama in Adult Education*[37] The ninth in the series, *Pioneer Work and Other Developments* (1927), contains the section 'Special Problems of the Countryside' which refers back to the 1922 document:

> *... It is a source of great satisfaction that so many of the difficulties have been removed, and so much development brought about, by means which were suggested or endorsed in that Report. In particular, Rural Community Councils have multiplied under the stimulus of the National Council of Social Service ... and in many counties have consolidated their position and have greatly extended the range of their work.*[38]

The inter-war period saw the greatest developments in large regional rural programmes by all providers. The universities instituted comprehensive geographical coverage of their 'Responsible Body' regions, with directors[39] and strategically-located resident tutors (as advocated by the 1919 Committee, and the WEA) evolving parallel district organisations with organising staff. By this process, for example, the extra-mural department of Southampton, founded in 1928, organised provision in central-southern England (West Sussex, Hampshire and East Dorset). A Director was appointed in 1930, and a full staff of resident tutors in the outlying areas to serve the villages of North Hampshire and Dorset. Similarly, Newcastle (then a college of the University of Durham) became the Responsible Body for Northumberland and Cumberland. No Director was appointed in the 1920s, but a Secretary was employed from 1926.

The amount of provision was not great in the early years. In 1924–5 Newcastle organised six one-year extension courses and 16 three-year tutorial classes, this rising to peaks of 37 extension courses in 1934–5 and 40 tutorial classes in 1947–8. The development of Newcastle as a provider for a large rural region followed conventional lines; a Director and full-time staff tutors were appointed, with a Resident Tutor appointed in Cumberland and a second Cumberland appointment made in 1949. A comparison with other university extra-mural departments for the years 1932–3 and 1937–8 shows

Newcastle to be a fairly typical provider. The number of grant-aided extension courses offered during this period by each university for its region is as follows:[40]

Cambridge	189
London	326
Newcastle	197
Nottingham	176
Oxford	113
Southampton	136

The subjects covered followed national trends. The early popularity of economics and politics gradually declined, while literature, philosophy and the arts in general were consistently in demand.

The development of university provision in Wales and Scotland was very slow in the early days of the tutorial classes. However, in the inter-war period there was a flourishing of both tutorial and the shorter extension courses in Wales, as well as vigorous provision by voluntary sector bodies such as the Welsh Council of YMCAs and the Welsh University Council of Music. By contrast, development remained slow in Scotland, with only limited provision in the rural areas as late as the outbreak of the Second World War.[41]

Post-war provision

The Second World War did not produce the policy-driven expansion which characterised the 1920s, and the 1944 Education Act did little to influence university provision. But the Act did place:

> ... firmly on the shoulders of LEAs the responsibility of securing adequate provision for further education [including] leisure-time occupation, and such organised cultural training and recreative activities as are suited to their requirements, for any persons over compulsory school age who are able and willing to profit by the facilities provided for that purpose.[42]

The war was followed by a rapid expansion in provision by the LEAs and the Responsible Bodies. Extra-mural departments made many full-time appointments, the numbers trebling between 1945 and 1951.[43] But within this expansion, rural provision by the universities suffered a decline as a result of a major policy debate about standards in the early 1950s. The difficulty of maintaining the flagship tutorial classes in small communities necessitated programmes of what were seen as the more lightweight courses of one term or shorter. Village students were also seen as unselective, since a reasonable choice of subject could not be offered and students would attend the one available class, whatever the subject. This situation could easily be attacked in any debate on standards.[44] This debate took place in the early 1950s. It was centred on the definitions of quality and standards, and whether there was a university standard to which all programmes, extra-mural included, must adhere. The main antagonists were S. G. Raybould of Leeds and Robert Peers of Nottingham.[45]

The effect of this 'great debate' was a change in programme policy which weakened rural provision. The argument was that standards of a demonstrable parity with internal undergraduate courses could not be maintained in rural classes, which were often jointly organised with the WEA. Therefore programmes and tutors would not achieve the status which the extra-mural directors of the day were seeking. The alternative argument was that it was a perfectly justifiable role of a university to respond to regional community needs alongside its national and international roles.

Depending on how they aligned with these arguments, a number of universities changed the character of their programmes; from extended rural outreach to concentration in adult education centres and colleges within urban or campus boundaries. Others (particularly those with large rural regions, such as Newcastle, Exeter, Nottingham and Cambridge) maintained the rural provision – though here too the programmes reflected the standards issue.

On the other hand, the agents for growth in rural provision at this time – particularly in the 1960s – were the local authorities. Funding policies based on student numbers encouraged new developments. County authorities reflected the popularity of urban outreach by an equivalent rural provision. In some authorities (for example, Hampshire and Leicestershire[46]) ambitious county-wide structures of staff and centres were established. But it has to be admitted that, for all this, the needs of rural scattered communities found comparatively little voice amid the increasingly vigorous developments of education for urban disadvantage.

By the end of the 1960s, assumptions about what characterised rural needs, and provision expressly to meet those needs, were becoming increasingly difficult to maintain. Village life was changing rapidly with the exodus to towns, owing to agriculture becoming less labour-intensive, and the parallel immigration to villages of professional people seeking rural domesticity. These changes in the demography of village life led to what the Redcliffe-Maud Royal Commission Report of 1969[47] referred to as the 'blurring' of the distinction between town and country. This view is summarised in a conference paper of 1974 on the topic of research into rural provision:

> ... increased mobility as a result of car ownership, a movement of people from the towns into the villages, a steady decline in the number of farmworkers, changes in educational provision which have either reduced the significance of or removed altogether the village school, and the spread of television viewing ... these changes have weakened the distinctive cultural characteristics of rural communities so that they are now only residual. From the point of view of adult education, the question arises whether much survives that is noticeably rural to investigate?[48]

Certainly these views are corroborated by various published reports. The National Institute for Adult Education (NIAE) report, *Adequacy of Provision*, commissioned by the Department of Education and Science in 1966,[49] found no reason to distinguish the rural from the urban population, even though four of the five areas surveyed had large agricultural areas. But the proportion of the labour force employed in agriculture had changed radically since the 1920s. Dorset, 'essentially a farming county',[50] now had only ten per cent of the labour force in agricultural work. Other publications in the late 1960s repeated the claim that the rural community no longer required special treatment – and indeed that tourism was bringing prosperity to remote communities and that provision should be targeted at the visitors.

Thereafter, issues of rural provision were related to the small size or remoteness of communities rather than any especial rurality of identity or dependence on agriculture. It was increasingly the developing world that attracted the attention of adult educators. The Russell Report[51] in 1973 identified problems including transport and accommodation. But unlike the reports of five decades before, Russell did not find any culture of resistance to education by villagers or their employers. The report suggested possible solutions to these problems, including the design of village schools as multi-purpose premises.

By the 1960s, a new approach to the problem of rural remoteness and scattered population was evolving – for instance, the use of radio and television as educational media to support flexible open learning.[52] Experiments were conducted using the new network of local radio stations, and the idea of learning groups with broadcast and tutorial support gained considerable favour. The initiatives ranged from a television vocational course for dairy farmers to liberal adult education by local radio in Cumbria.[53] Conferences were held in a mood of optimism – about, for example, 'the contribution that the mass media can make to rural adult education and to rural communities.'[54] These initiatives did not get beyond the experimental stage, but did indicate a possible future solution to the intractable problem of remote and scattered communities.

The published report of one such conference in 1978, addressing rural provision in East Anglia, is interestingly revealing of the changes in definition of the target groups for the rural adult educator, and thus of the perceived character of the rural village population: 'conservation workers, amenity societies, housewives and farm workers.' No ranking in these categories was intended, but perhaps some inference can be drawn from the position of agricultural workers in the list.[55]

The large changes in the organisation of adult education in the 1980s – the drastic reduction in LEA-organised provision, the reductions in staff of the Responsible Bodies, especially the erosion of resident tutor/tutor organiser posts in the regional outstations – had a deleterious effect on rural provision. Programmes dwindled in size and seriousness as the organising staff retreated to the campuses and towns. Most university CE departments reduced their rural outreach. Joint provision with WEA village branches, which had been the mainstay of much of this work, was badly affected by the reduction in both the number of rural branches and loss of university resident tutor posts.

The bringing of university CE programmes within the mainstream of credit-based funding in 1994–5 aggravated this situation. The necessary higher levels of accountability and administration were burdensome to the many voluntary local organisers. Changes in village student profiles – for example, a high proportion of well-qualified retired people – lessened the perceived relevance and appeal of accreditation. On the other hand, the special project funding for widening provision emerging from these changes led to a number of initiatives for rural outreach targeted at geographical areas of particular need; for example, Shropshire, Fenland and Northumberland.

National bodies and rural provision

National adult education organisations have taken note of rural problems from the start. In 1926 the first edition of the journal *Adult Education* carried an article on administrative problems of rural provision.[56] The varying frequency of such articles over the life of this journal is an indicator of the level of concern or activity amongst practitioners. The WEA reports on (or partly on) rural issues have been mentioned. The Standing Conference on University Teaching and Research in the Education of Adults (SCUTREA) included it on the agenda of its fourth annual conference in 1974.[57]

To scrutinise the reports of government and other national organisations is to observe the dwindling of the significance of 'rural' as a descriptor for an understood area of educational need or provision. The NIAE *Adequacy of Provision* report of 1970 marks the watershed beyond which 'rural' is not of itself significant. A review of the several recent major reports confirms this trend. The reports of Dearing, Kennedy, Fryer and the government Green Paper, *The Learning Age*[58], all address disadvantage, the need for the removal of barriers to access and the needs of 'those living in isolated or remote locations.' But 'rural' does not figure in the vocabulary. Indeed, it would seem that there is no concept of 'rurality' as cognate with any image of a significant segment of the population with a recognisable set of educational needs, or (significantly) embodying an economic and political imperative. On the other hand, the government White Paper, *Our Countryside: The Future*[59] published in November 2000, addresses rural issues but without any substantial treatment of lifelong learning in the rural context. Ironically, only a few weeks after its publication the 2001 outbreak of Foot and Mouth disease precipitated a need for rural lifelong education and training of a scale and urgency unprecedented since the 1920s.

The Universities Council for Adult Education, established in 1947 and now the Universities Association for Continuing Education (UACE), regularly included rural issues in its reports and agendas, but it has only recently implemented perhaps the most consistent and vigorous national overview of rural provision in the form of its Rural Network, founded in 1996. This network of practitioners has kept the issues facing rural provision in the consciousness of UACE and thereby in the policy and funding debates at national level. The post-mainstream funding for rural projects has been a unique example of higher education funding expressly directed to combat rural educational disadvantage.[60]

Indeed the problems facing rural provision need to be kept in full view, and must not be obscured by the changes in rural life over the last forty years. The large immigration of middle-class, urban dwellers, who strive to recreate a village community based on a pastoral rather than a real or even historical model, has been reflected in the provision of adult education. This is, most typically, campus provision located in the country rather than provision designed for identified rural community needs. This is a great change from the economic imperatives of the 1920s, when the experience of blockade led government to invest in the education, training and welfare of agricultural workers. The present-day indigenous rural economy is in a marginal and fragmented condition, with agriculture representing less than two per cent of gross domestic product.

Of course rural disadvantage has by no means been eradicated, and it could be argued that it is once again increasing. Reduced public transport and difficulty of access to electronic communication would exemplify this tendency. Postcode-based identification of disadvantage is unreliable in rural areas, while identification of educational need and provision to meet that need are both relatively expensive compared to urban equivalents. Funding and quality methodologies can be unhelpful to the rural learner. In the current climate it is essential that the less advantaged rural communities are not excluded from the widening participation culture. There should be no return to the haphazard educational opportunity outlined at the start of this chapter.

Conclusion

Except in communities (mainly mining) that were touched by the university extension movement, rural adult education remained undeveloped in comparison to its urban counterpart until the end of the nineteenth century. The 1870 Education Act exposed the problems of educational provision in isolated and scattered communities. By the early years of the twentieth century the problems of rural deprivation and the consequent drift of able young people to towns were recognised. The real impetus to rural provision for adults followed the Great War, with the recommendations of the Ministry of Reconstruction report (the '1919 Report') leading directly to the comprehensive adult education set up from the 1920s by universities, the WEA, and later the LEAs. This development continued after 1945, assisted by an increase in full-time university staff and the enhanced role of the LEAs after the 1944 Act.

In the 1960s, the changes in rural demography led to a redefinition of 'rural' needs. With the continuing decline in agricultural employment, and villages increasingly becoming dormitories for commuters, retirement homes and tourism, the emphasis changed from an assumed rural disadvantage to an abolition of the rural-urban distinction. This attitude was strengthened by the parallel rise in adult educators' interest in rural education in the less developed world.

The 1980s saw a further decline in traditional rural employment, and in public transport. This led to a renewal of the concept of particular social and educational disadvantage in rural communities. The rhetoric of government and research reports changed from a concept of rurality to one of exclusion and access. The exponential rise in communications technology, so characteristic of this period, can be seen as both a great opportunity for access to CE for isolated individuals and communities, but also as a further barrier to learning for those without access to networked computers. These and other issues have been the focus of projects by the UACE Rural Network, funded by the Higher Education Funding Council for England, for enabling rural communities to engage in the lifelong learning agenda. In the aftermath of the 2001 Foot and Mouth disease epidemic and its impact on rural life, work and economy, this is once again at a critical defining moment.

Notes

1. For a convenient source of information on Duck and Collier, see Thompson, E.P. (1989). *'The Thresher's Labour' by Stephen Duck, 'The Woman's Labour' by Mary Collier; Two Eighteenth Century Poems.* The Merlin Press.
2. Collier, M. (1762). *Some Remarks on the Author's Life* (autobiographical memoir) prefaced to *Poems on Several Occasions.*
3. A convenient edition with an introduction is Mack, D.S. ed. (1970). *James Hogg; Selected Poems.* Clarendon.
4. See Kelly, T. (1992). *A History of Adult Education in Great Britain.* Liverpool University Press; pp. 66–68.
5. *Ibid.*, p. 69, cites Jones, M.G. (1938). *The Charity School Movement in the XVIII Century*; Cambridge University Press; p. 210.
6. There were exceptions, or 'reasonable excuses' applying, for example, if there was no public elementary school within three miles by the nearest road.
7. Warner, P.W. (1973). Rural education. In *Aspects of Education No 17.* University of Hull, Institute of Education; p. 6.
8. Roberts, R.D. (1891). *Eighteen Years of University Extension.* Cambridge University Press; p. 26.
9. *Ibid.*, p. 46.
10. *Ibid.*, p. 48.
11. *Ibid.*, p. 50.
12. *Ibid.*, p. 49.
13. Sadler, M.E. (1907). *Continuation Schools in England and Elsewhere: Their Place in the Educational System of an Industrial and Commercial State.* Manchester; p. 714.
14. WEA. (1918). *Education Year Book*; pp. 352–3.

15.   Ministry of Reconstruction (1919). *The Final and Interim Reports of the Adult Education Committee*. HMSO. Reprint: University of Nottingham, Department of Adult Education, 1980.

16.   *Ibid., Interim Report. Industrial and social conditions in relation to adult education*; p. 84.

17.   *Ibid.*, p. 86.

18.   *Ibid.*, p. 87.

19.   *Ibid., Final Report*, p. 262.

20.   *Ibid., Interim Report*, p. 87.

21.   *Ibid.*, p. 87.

22.   *Ibid.*, pp. 142–3.

23.   *Ibid.*, p. 147.

24.   *Times Educational Supplement*, 13 December 1924. Quoted in Ree, H. (1973). *Educator Extraordinary: The Life and Achievements of Henry Morris*. Longman; p. 22.

25.   Board of Education (1922). *The Development of Adult Education in Rural Areas. A Report by the Adult Education Committee of the Board of Education*. Paper no. 3; HMSO.

26.   *Ibid.*, p. 1.

27.   *Ibid.*, passim.

28.   *Ibid.*, p. 4.

29.   *Ibid.*, p. 3.

30.   *Ibid.*, p. 6.

31.   *Ibid.*, p. 32.

32.   *Ibid.*, p. 10.

33.   *Ibid.*, pp. 10–11.

34.   *Ibid.*, p. 35.

35.   Morris, H. (1925). *The Village College, being a Memorandum on the Provision of Educational and Social Facilities for the Countryside, with Special Reference to Cambridge*. Cambridge, 2nd. edn. In Ree, *op cit.*, pp. 143–57.

36.   Ree, *op. cit.*, p. 153.

37.   Board of Education (1926). *The Drama in Adult Education. A Report by the Adult Education Committee of the Board of Education*. Paper no 6. HMSO. See 'The Drama in the Countryside', pp. 298–348. The 1922 report had recommended drama as an activity to be fostered in rural provision, and indeed it has a distinguished history as an activity in rural adult education. There were many well-supported initiatives in villages, some of which gave rise to amateur theatres which survive today. The Village Drama Society had 150 branches and was active in 2000 villages. There was a particularly innovative and successful programme in Lancashire in the post-war years.

38.   Board of Education (1927). *Pioneer Work and Other Developments in Adult Education. A Report by the Adult Education Committee of the Board*

of Education. Paper No 9. HMSO; pp. 55–56.

39 The first appointed Director was Robert Peers at Nottingham in 1920. He was appointed Professor in 1922, again the first in the country.

40 Raybould, S.G. (1951). *The English Universities and Adult Education.* WEA; p. 159.

41. Kelly, *op. cit.*, p. 273.

42. *Ibid.*, p. 337.

43. Fieldhouse, R. *et al.* (1996). *A History of Modern British Adult Education.* NIACE; p. 212.

44. Armstrong, J.R. (1947). *The rural class: a problem of standards.* Typescript in possession of WRJ; p. 3.

45. The key texts in the 'great debate' are: Raybould, S.G. (1951). *The English Universities and Adult Education.* WEA; Peers, R. (1952). The future of adult education. *Adult Education*, vol. 25, no. 2, Autumn; pp. 87–95; Raybould, S.G. (1952). Standards or quality. *Adult Education*, vol. 25, no. 3, Winter; pp. 172–9; Waller, R.D. (1953). The great debate. *Adult Education*, vol. 25, no. 4, Spring; pp. 250–63. For a defence of standards and quality in rural university classes see Armstrong, J.R. (1952). Liberal adult education in rural areas: a plea for the village. *Adult Education*, vol. 25, no. 1, Summer; pp. 56–62.

46. For an account of the Leicestershire scheme see Fairbairn, A.N. (1978). *The Leicestershire Community Colleges and Centres.* University of Nottingham Department of Adult Education.

47. Royal Commission on Local Government in England, 1966–9. Presented to Parliament by command of Her Majesty, June 1969.

48. Styler, W.E. (1974). Research into rural adult education. Standing Conference on University Teaching and Research in the Education of Adults. (SCUTREA) *Papers from the Fourth Annual Conference.*

49. National Institute of Adult Education (1970). *Adequacy of Provision.*

50. *Ibid.*, p. 25.

51. Department of Education & Science (1973). *Adult Education: A Plan for Development.* (The Russell Report), HMSO

52. Experiments in broadcast media and adult education began in the 1920s when the BBC set up listening groups for education by radio. This was hailed as a good way to reach village populations, but in fact success was very limited and it had died out by 1939.

53. Howell, J. (1968). *Educational Television for Farmers.* University of Reading, Agricultural Extension Centre; West, L. (1979). Continuing education and local radio in Cumbria. *Adult Education*, vol. 52, no. 3; pp. 185–6.

54. National Extension College/Chelmer Institute of Higher Education (1979). Rural adult education workshop report. *National Extension College Report 5*, series 2, no. 5.

55. *Ibid.*, p. 2. In Norfolk in 1976 agricultural workers represented 20 per

cent of the 62,000 people employed in the rural areas.

56. *Journal of Adult Education* (1926). vol. 1, no. 1. British Institute for Adult Education; pp. 100–8.

57. Styler, *op. cit.*

58. The reports are: National Committee for Enquiry into Higher Education (1997). *Higher Education in the Learning Society.* (The Dearing Report), HMSO; The Further Education Funding Council (1997). *Learning Works: Widening Participation in Further Education.* (The Kennedy Report), FEFC; National Advisory Group for Continuing Education and Lifelong Learning (1997). *Learning for the Twenty-first Century.* (The Fryer Report), Department for Education and Employment; Department for Education and Employment (1998). *The Learning Age: A Renaissance for a New Britain.*

59. DETR (2000). *Our Countryside: The Future - A Fair Deal for Rural England.* Cm 4909.

60. There are, of course, many non-HEFCE-funded programmes for rural access to education, one example being the Northumberland Village Access initiative for women in rural communities.

Part 2

5

Combating rural social exclusion: adult guidance and lifelong learning in Mid and West Wales

Sue Pester

Background and context

Social inclusion is now a priority issue on the UK political agenda and is perceived to be a prerequisite to economic regeneration. The reasons for and characteristics of social exclusion vary in different contexts but poverty, lack of education and unemployment are generally recognised as key factors. Poverty is understood as an experience that extends beyond immediate material deprivation. Paid work not only connects people to formal and informal social structures but also promotes a sense of identity and self-worth. Those who are outside the world of work can thereby be outside the social and economic structures and networks that sustain much of modern life. Lack of education and unemployment can contribute to isolation, low self-esteem and a lack of confidence. Cycles of exclusion and their relationship to low participation in post-compulsory education and training has been well researched and documented over recent years.[1] In rural areas, where amenities and public services are more difficult to access on a low income, the experience of isolation may be more intense and more damaging.

Mid Wales is a sparsely populated rural area with a population density of 0.26 persons per hectare, compared with an all-Wales average of 1.4.[2] It continues to be heavily dependent on agriculture, but the decline of that industry, exacerbated by events such as the BSE crisis, Common Agricultural Policy reforms, an ageing farming community and the recent strength of the pound, has had a serious affect upon farmers and food manufacturers.[3] Employment is dominated by the service sector and the average gross weekly earnings for full-time employees (£319.40) lags significantly behind that of Wales as a whole (£353.60), with areas such as Ceredigion being as low as £275.80.[4] There is a high level of low-paid, seasonal employment.

The lack of services, particularly public transport, combined with unemployment and low-paid employment results in multiple disadvantage for many people. However, government policies tend to relate 'disadvantage' to urban poverty while 'rural' conjures up images of peace and well-being. The reality is that 25 per cent of rural families may be living on, or below, the poverty line.[5] Recent research has identified the urgent need to recognise the extent of social exclusion and poverty in Mid Wales and to develop a national set of indicators relating to rural disadvantage.[6]

A series of Welsh Office Papers has identified a growing skills 'deficit' in Wales and highlighted the link between learning and economic prosperity. The 1998 *Learning Is For Everyone* (LIFE) Green Paper produced some alarming statistics in relation to the low level of skills and current learning in Wales. For example:

- 370,000 adults of working age have no qualifications;
- Over 90 per cent of the population (aged 16 years and over) are not enrolled on adult education courses;
- Over two-fifths of the working age population have low numeracy skills;
- One in six of the working age population have low reading skills;
- Overall, Wales lags behind other parts of the UK and our overseas competitors in developing basic and intermediate skills.

Exclusion and guidance

One of the immediate concerns for higher education (HE) institutions relating to social exclusion is the widening of access to groups which are under-represented in HE. There is also an increasing focus on the regional mission of universities and their responsibility for supporting the local and national economy through wealth-generation and community capacity-building activities. The role of continuing education (CE)/lifelong learning in serving those who would not normally participate in HE has become of increasing interest to universities and politicians.

The 1997 Dearing Report identified the potential role of careers education and guidance in relation to widening access, and suggested further development of the service: 'The government, in the medium- to long-term, should integrate careers advice for lifelong learning, to complement services based inside HE institutions.'[7] Similarly LIFE states: 'We believe that everyone should have ready access to high-quality, impartial careers information, including information on learning opportunities in informal settings or through distance and open learning.'[8]

This chapter examines issues relating to adult guidance and social exclusion in Mid and West Wales and seeks to identify the potential role of guidance activity, organised and managed by centres of CE/lifelong learning. It makes reference to existing provision and research at the University of Wales, Aberystwyth (UWA).

The UWA Adult Guidance Service was developed in the context of an increasingly explicit regional mission for HE. Although it could be argued that this has always been the case, the demand for universities to become more explicitly involved in their regional economies has become greater. The 1998

Education and Training Action Plan for Wales (ETAP)[9] identified the essential role of education and training in relation to economic and social development and emphasised the need to strengthen the adult careers guidance service.

Guidance, like education, is now recognised as a process that continues throughout life rather than something that happens at a particular stage in youth. Changes in the labour market and the rapid development of new forms of information have resulted in a different attitude to employment. A job for life is now the exception rather than the norm and young people no longer expect to have one career. Rather, they expect to manage successive careers and to make changes, including the acquisition of new knowledge, when necessary.

Adult guidance is an important issue in debates about social exclusion and widening participation, being one means by which providers can contact and motivate those least likely to access educational opportunities. In a major survey of access to vocational guidance for people at risk of social exclusion, Pamela Clayton identifies the most at-risk groups as those that:

- live in rural or deprived areas
- are unemployed or in low-paid insecure employment
- have disabilities
- are members of ethnic minorities, refugees or Travellers
- are homeless or ex-offenders.[10]

In Wales, the funding for adult guidance comes from the European Union (EU) via the National Assembly (previously the Welsh Office), and was routed through the Training and Enterprise Councils (TECs). In April 2001, responsibility for adult guidance was transferred to the newly-established Careers Wales. The EU focuses its attention on areas of disadvantage and on individuals within those regions who are deemed to be particularly disadvantaged. There is a significant variation in the provision of adult guidance services between different European countries, and sometimes within individual member states. In the UK, guidance for young people remains a statutory responsibility administered through the careers companies, while services for adults remain non-statutory and uneven.[11]

The Adult Guidance Initiative started in 1993, and later the five, then four, TECs in Wales, jointly launched an all-Wales approach to the development of the service, including agreed quality standards. Various providers were able to bid for funds to deliver aspects of the service or to deliver to particular target groups. While the majority of the available resources went to the careers companies, HE, further education (FE) and other providers, such as youth drop-in centres could apply for appropriate funding on an annual basis to support their services. This approach has enabled the development of a particular type of guidance service, one that is delivered in the community through projects designed and supported by community groups.

In relation to Welsh HE, an element of the block grant includes the provision of careers guidance. The only area where this cannot be identified is in relation to non-award-bearing (widening access) provision. Institutions can therefore legitimately request funding to support guidance activities for those people enrolled on this type of provision.

The potential role of the guidance worker

Guidance is sometimes perceived as having two distinct strands: vocational adult guidance that supports access into the labour market, and educational guidance that enables individuals to make informed choices about educational and training opportunities. The UWA project is based on the practice of providing adult guidance within the community, using a holistic, client-centred approach. No attempt is made to distinguish between vocational or educational needs. Personal development through problem-solving and decision-making is a central aim of the service. It is also underpinned by the understanding that an impartial, professional and confidential guidance service is as much a prerequisite for a successful adult education provision as it is for a successful economy.

The types of services offered through UWA include information and signposting activities. These are directly available through the non-award-bearing provision and are relatively straightforward. 'Students' become 'clients' and are offered initial information and advice, or are referred to other provision, other agencies or to a more in-depth and focussed guidance interview. The transition from community education to guidance is seamless, but this process must ensure that the client is central to the situation. A second service offered by UWA is individual interviews to assist clients in identifying long-term goals and strategies for their achievement. This can be a long process with clients sometimes remaining in contact with the guidance worker for several months, returning at intervals for further sessions.

Both types of service are available within the community and can be accessed through the non-award-bearing, non-vocational CE provision. Within these two broad strands, guidance practitioners would identify the following nine activities as essential to a professional service:

> **Informing**: Guidance workers should have access to significant amounts of information, in electronic or paper format, relating to learning opportunities in the region and elsewhere. The information must be presented to the clients in an impartial manner.

> **Advising**: Clients often need help in identifying their needs and interpreting the available information, but this does not involve making choices for the client.

> **Facilitating**: Clients often require considerable time to identify and understand their own needs and to evaluate ways in which

these can be met. They may be unclear about their requirements and need time to consider their options.

Assessing: Clients often lack confidence and are unaware of their existing skills, or the skills/knowledge that they will need to acquire to achieve their aims. Unless clients are in an informed position, they are unable to make reliable choices about their future.

Enabling: Clients often need support and encouragement; for example, to contact government agencies, complete complicated forms or to identify the right person to provide necessary information.

Advocating: Occasionally it is necessary to contact other agencies directly, particularly in a crisis situation or where there are additional barriers, such as lack of competence in the English language.

Feeding back: The guidance workers will communicate back to the client issues that have been identified and decisions that have been made. This enables the client to clarify his/her assessment of the situation, his/her goals and the necessary steps that have been identified. A different feedback process involves analysing data and communicating back to the providing organisation (or network of organisations) details of educational, training and employment opportunities that are being sought. For example, there may be an identifiable demand for more information technology (IT) courses in a particular geographical area, or for more part-time provision in FE or HE.

Teaching: As a group activity, this targets specific groups identified as having particular barriers to access. It seeks to enable participants to gain the necessary skills, confidence and knowledge to make informed choices. UWA has had funding support from the TECs (and more recently Education and Learning Wales) for this type of teaching, targeting:

- women with young children
- ethnic minority groups
- young, unemployed men.

Networking: One of the most valuable aspects of guidance is the opportunity to communicate with a range of education and training providers. This enables guidance workers to have up-to-date information about existing or planned provision offered by other organisations and facilitates effective referrals between organisations.

One of the key issues for the guidance practitioner is to understand, accept and adhere to the parameters of the service offered. Whist this is clearly explained to the client at the beginning of the interview, an enquiry concerning educational or training opportunities can rapidly develop into a personal counselling situation for which the guidance worker may not be equipped, trained nor employed to deliver. To close the door on the client, at a point when they may be particularly vulnerable or in need, is equally unprofessional and potentially very damaging. In this situation the guidance worker would carefully agree a referral to an appropriate agency with the client, offering support to make the necessary arrangements. It would then be important to 'wind down' the guidance session in a supportive manner; for example, by summarising the meeting and engaging the client in casual conversation.

For many people, guidance will be prompted by some particular life event. Many interviews coincide with birthdays and others with relationship breakdowns or changes in employment status. Thus guidance is frequently sought at a time when the client is particularly vulnerable and can provide crucial support during a process of transition. However, the process of guidance is not intended to be fortune-telling. Instead it aims to place the individual at the centre of decision-making, encouraging autonomy and enabling the client to take control of their learning, and ultimately their life. It therefore links in very naturally with notions of citizenship and empowerment. A successful guidance interview should raise aspirations and motivate. The decision-making processes are vital. It is not unusual to meet a client who believes that all the decisions affecting their life, to date, have been made by other people. This can lead to feelings of disempowerment and, ultimately, to alienation from society.

The manner in which the process of client-centred guidance has developed owes much to the work of Carl Rogers and links to theoretical perspectives of the process of learning. Recent discourse in CE has identified the value of learner autonomy. There has been a distinct shift in educational practice towards putting the learner, rather than the lecturer or tutor, at the centre of the learning process.

Jackson and Haughton identify the distinctive features and benefits of community-based guidance as:

- Being undertaken within a broader agenda of individual health and personal development, often addressing a number of different, but related needs.

- Being delivered by practitioners whose remit with clients is often much broader and wider-ranging than just guidance for learning or work.
- Approaches that prioritise:
  - outreach
  - befriending
  - discretion and confidentiality
  - advocacy (as appropriate)
  - individual attention to special needs
  - ongoing support and accessibility
  - no charge.

Above all, approaches are relaxed and informal, are totally voluntary and usually take place at venues people already go to, are familiar with, and are non-threatening.[12]

It is this informal, flexible and welcoming character of the provision that makes it particularly accessible to people from lower socio-economic groups. Many, perhaps the majority, who use the service would not visit an agency offering careers guidance as they do not have a 'career'. Indeed the very word may be alien to them. Some people are also suspicious of government agencies. The result is that the people who would most benefit from guidance are those who are least likely to access it. The Kennedy Report recognised this:

> It would be true to say that, at present, anyone who wants initial advice and guidance can generally get it. The snag is that they need to have the self-confidence and awareness of what is available to seek it out and to present themselves for it. Potential learners who are outside the magic circle of education and training where it is provided get the worst deal of all.[13]

Recent University for Industry (UfI)-type initiatives are attempting to address this problem but it is clear that a wide range of initiatives and providers are required to ensure that the service is as accessible as possible. In particular, the need for outreach infrastructure within communities must be highlighted if adult guidance is to reach those who would most gain from it.

Putting guidance into practice

The adult guidance service at UWA is delivered through the Lifelong Learning Office responsible for the non-award-bearing, non-vocational CE provision. While it may be argued that the guidance is targeting people already within learning situations, it should be stressed that the non-award-bearing provision is itself aimed at non-participating groups. The office works with community groups to identify ways in which education and training initiatives can support capacity-building projects and widen access to HE.

One such project is the Penparcau Partnership, based in two locations on a housing estate on the outskirts of the town. The known characteristics of the area include various indicators of social deprivation and exclusion. There is a high percentage of single parents, a significant number of non-car-owning families (though it is accepted that not owning a car is not a reliable indicator of exclusion in rural areas) and a low participation rate in HE and FE. The project targets women with pre-school-age children and the long-term unemployed. The Family Centre, situated in the heart of the estate, makes a vital contribution to the partnership. The Centre is a drop-in, information and support agency. It consists of two interconnecting houses and has been used this year by 69 women, seven men and 123 children. It includes a crèche and a training room, both of which are made freely available to the project. Courses are offered on a diverse range of subjects, including creative writing, Shiatsu, beginners' Welsh, diet and healthy lifestyle and conflict resolution.

The curriculum is responsive to the needs of the community and recent requests have been made for basic IT and more provision relating to alternative therapies. Students attending these classes were not previously participating in learning – nor were they likely to do so unless the provision was accessible (geographically and as a non-threatening location), affordable (free of charge) and had good-quality childcare. At present, all those participating are women. The majority have no formal qualifications and there is a higher than average number of lone parents and long-term (three or more years) unemployment. Full- or part-time members of UWA staff teach the courses. Some part-time staff are also able to make a significant input to the project's resource-base through private, lottery and other sources of funding. This commitment to partnership is essential, as the provision is expensive and can only be delivered through pooling the resources of the various partners. Penparcau has been identified as qualifying for inclusion within the Assembly's Community First initiative, enabling a more intense level of support to be provided.

Another partnership project involves working with young unemployed people (mainly but not exclusively young men) through a drop-in centre at Cardigan. Staff from the centre and community trainers working for UWA have devised a curriculum which assists in the development of basic social and communication skills. The participants are taken to a specially chosen venue and spend the day engaged in a variety of activities designed to improve confidence and feelings of self-worth and to support the acquisition of new skills.

Research into community development and regeneration in rural Wales highlights the value of strategies involving community partnerships, not simply to enlarge the resource base but also to enable local communities to share in the strategy and decision-making processes.[14]

Guidance is offered at a stage when participants are thought most likely to benefit, usually towards the end of a course or a series of courses. It is provided at a convenient time, in a familiar location (such as the Family Centre) and is entirely optional. The service consists of a small team of professionally trained and qualified staff who are not involved in the delivery of the non-award-bearing provision. The service is free, confidential and impartial. The process helps the client to identify goals and the ways in which these can be achieved. Both existing skills, experience and qualifications and 'gaps' or barriers to achievement are identified, leading to an agreed action plan. Information about available education and training opportunities are accessed through laptop computers using, in particular, the Training and Information Services (TIS) database and paper-based information. A wide range of information is available on FE, HE, the Workers' Educational Association (WEA), voluntary and community-based provision and local childcare. Financial and childcare matters are the issues that feature most prominently, and both client and staff feedback is analysed regularly in order to identify trends and to improve the service.

The code of practice underpinning the service includes a commitment to impartiality, confidentiality, individual ownership, equal opportunities, transparency and accessibility. It is recognised that barriers to such provision may exist. For example, impartiality may be limited, albeit unconsciously, by personal or social factors relating to the guidance worker, or more consciously, by the needs of the providing institution. Resources and the availability of venues may limit accessibility. However, a commitment is made to adhere as closely as possible to these principles through ongoing training, monitoring and reviewing.

The guidance process as a vehicle for developing skills

Action planning is becoming widely used within education, training and employment situations and is increasingly used in schools. The guidance interview involves aiding the development of important interpersonal and transferable skills. It provides a safe environment for reviewing the past, examining the present and identifying realistic goals for the future. The client is supported and encouraged to identify her or his needs, explore options and identify barriers to achievement. These may be relatively straightforward and involve, for example, the selection of an appropriate course. However, the client's needs are often more complex and may relate to family finances, childcare or deep-seated anxieties and/or lack of confidence. Many clients underestimate their own level of skills because these have been acquired through informal learning. To identify and name skills involved in, for example, managing a home and children, can be a very empowering experience. Jacquie MacDonald identifies the following questions as a reflection of the skills development integral to the process:

- Where am I now in terms of achievement? (self-awareness)
- What are my aims? (decision making + opportunity awareness)
- What do I need to do in order to achieve my aims? (decision making)
- What support do I need? (interpersonal skills + decision making)
- What timescale am I talking about? (transition skills)
- What action do I take? (self-awareness + decision making)
- How am I doing? Is there a need to review my aims? (self-awareness, decision making skills + transition skills).[15]

As already stated, skills development is very high on the agenda of FE and HE institutions. A 1999 survey (Table 1) identified the views of employers in each of the regions of Wales on priority skill areas:[16]

Table 1. Skill requirements of employers (per cent of employers stating that a particular skill is very important to their needs)

Skill-type	Mid Wales	South East Wales	West Wales	North Wales	All Wales
Communication skills	86	87	89	89	88
Understanding customer needs	90	87	90	88	88
Ability to learn	79	81	80	82	81
Team working skills	80	81	79	84	81
Showing initiative	81	79	78	83	80
Ability to follow instructions	82	77	81	81	79
Literacy	73	76	74	77	76
Numeracy	71	71	71	70	71
Product knowledge	72	70	72	73	71
Problem-solving skills	66	65	65	68	66
Organising own learning & development	54	56	61	59	58
Job-specific skills	56	57	55	58	57
Management skills	47	49	51	50	50
Leadership skills	44	45	45	47	45
Basic IT skills	35	42	36	39	39
Formal qualifications	22	26	23	23	24
Advanced IT skills	16	18	15	16	16
Welsh language skills	20	3	13	19	11
Foreign language skills	4	4	4	4	4

The findings reveal that interpersonal and transferable skills are far more highly valued by employers than job-specific skills. (The high value attached to 'Understanding customer needs' may reflect the heavy dependence on the service sector in Mid Wales.) If the process of guidance can encourage the development of these skills then ultimately not only the individual but also the regional economy may benefit.

Reflecting on outcomes

Recent research within UWA has analysed a random sample of 935 Action Plans produced over the last three years and generated by the full range of non-award-bearing courses. The findings reveal the strong preponderance of women taking advantage of the guidance service (Figure 1). This represents 72 per cent and is slightly higher than the national average of women participating in part-time and evening-class provision.[17] Recent studies on gender and participation rates conclude that guidance in informal settings can be effective in attracting men into learning. To do so, the locations and the manner of contact may need careful planning, and may be quite different from the traditional, outreach community education courses. For male clients, venues such as sports centres, pubs and shopping malls are suggested as appropriate contact points for outreach guidance workers.[18]

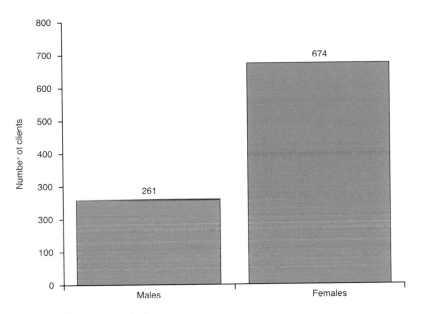

Figure 1. Gender of clients

The high percentage of women seeking education, training and employment reflects local and national employment patterns. Although, nationally, women constitute over 52 per cent of the labour market,[19] many are in low-paid, part-time and insecure employment. Girls now out-perform boys in school and more women access full-time HE than ever before. Nonetheless women are still considered to be particularly at risk of social exclusion.[20] One reason for this is that they are still regarded as the primary carers; and the difficulties surrounding affordable and accessible childcare creates significant barriers for women, particularly in rural areas. National studies reveal that 16 per cent of women cite childcare, or care for other dependants, as the main barrier to participating in learning – and this rises to 40 per cent for those with pre-school-aged children.[21] This is exacerbated by the fact that women are, on average, paid less than men.[22] In order to assist clients in identifying available childcare, the UWA guidance workers are provided with an electronic database of childcare opportunities. Information can be accessed by location, includes all registered child-minders and crèche/childcare centres and indicates whether the language spoken is English or Welsh.

Of those seeking guidance, 62 per cent are between the ages of 25–50 (Figure 2). Fifty three per cent are unemployed and, of those, about one third are long-term unemployed (Figure 3). Again, recent studies[23] have demonstrated that the unemployed are less likely than the employed to have been involved in recent learning and that they face particular barriers to employment. Clients report an erosion of motivation and confidence when out of paid work for long periods. Within this umbrella group there are many sub-groups, each with their own set of barriers – for example, young people, the homeless, people with disabilities and people living in rural areas. Guidance must be carefully targeted, well constructed and well delivered if it is to have any significant impact on these groups.

One of the most striking findings of the research is the looked-for progression identified by the clients (Figure 4). Over 73 per cent request information about vocational courses (excluding Welsh for Adults) while only 18 per cent are interested in academic or cultural courses. This indicates that the majority of

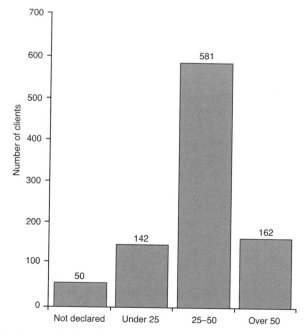

Figure 2. Age of clients

people using the service are looking to find employment or to improve their employment status. The service clearly relates to the social and economic needs of the communities and cannot be perceived simply as a means of promoting universities' provision.

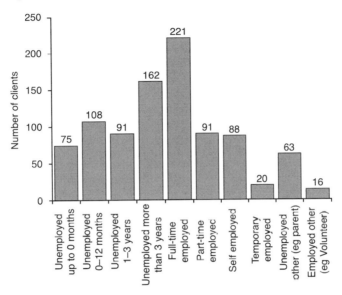

Figure 3. Employment status of clients

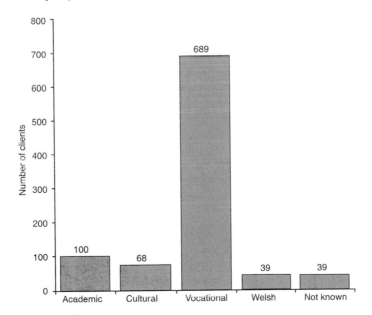

Figure 4. Type of course

Conclusion

There are many benefits from adult guidance, particularly the way in which it can contact those at risk of social exclusion. The community-based nature of the provision and the opportunities for effective partnerships and networking are essential to its effectiveness. Its location within HE enables the practitioners to benefit from relevant research generated by other parts of the institution in relation to policy and strategic developments. In return, the close contact with communities supports the institution in its regional mission and its efforts to widen access to groups and individuals that would not normally participate in education.

The nature of the project has been interventionist and, as such, it has directly impacted onto the lives of many people. The mobile and flexible nature of the guidance provision has enabled it to overcome many of the difficulties associated with rural areas. However the guidance interview and the resulting action plan should be the beginning of a longer process towards the achievement of a more fulfilling life. The reality is that it can be very difficult to access the available training, education or employment opportunities within rural areas. A limitation of the project has been the failure to engage in a follow-up study of clients after a period of time. Resources have not been available to support this activity and this has inhibited a full evaluation of the project.

The project has been facilitated by the partnerships formed with outside organisations, firstly through the co-ordination of West Wales TEC, then with Mid Wales TEC and more recently with Careers Wales (West). Without the support of these organisations the guidance activity at UWA would not have been possible. The project has also facilitated a closer relationship with the careers companies, voluntary groups and other educational providers. The shared objectives of regional regeneration and developing a sense of regional identity provide the crucial elements necessary for successful, long-term collaboration.

Acknowledgement

The author acknowledges the invaluable contribution of Anne Oldham, the university's Adult Guidance Worker, to the work described in this chapter.

Notes

1. Woodrow, M. *et al.* (1998). *From Elitism to Inclusion: Good Practice in Widening Access to Higher Education*. CVCP; Sargant, N. with Field, J., Francis, H., Schuller, T. and Tuckett, A. (1998). *The Learning Divide*. NIACE. See particularly the chapter on Wales by Hywel Francis.
2. Office for National Statistics, mid-year estimates, 1998.
3. Labour market information for Ceredigion and Mid Wales. *Mid Wales Skills Support*, July 2000.
4. *Ibid.*, p. 3.
5. Clayton, P. ed. (1999). *Access to Vocational Guidance for People at Risk of*

Social Exclusion, Leonardo Survey and Analysis 1996–8. Department of Adult and Continuing Education, University of Glasgow; February, p. 16.

6.   Goodwin, M., Edwards, B., Pemberton, S. and Woods, M. (1999). *Community action, partnerships and emergent forms of governance in rural Wales and the Borders.* Interim Report for the Joseph Rowntree Foundation Research Programme. Institute of Geography and Earth Studies, UWA. See also Edwards, B., Goodwin, M., Pemberton, S. and Woods, M. (2000). *Partnership Working in Rural Regeneration: Governance and Empowerment.* The Policy Press.

7.   National Committee for Enquiry into Higher Education (1997). *Higher Education in the Learning Society.* (The Dearing Report), HMSO; Recommendation 11.

8.   The Welsh Office, (1998). *Learning Is For Everyone (LIFE)*; p. 9.

9.   The Education and Training Action Group for Wales (1998). *An Education and Training Action Plan for Wales, Draft for Consultation.* Manweb Plc.

10.   Clayton, *op. cit.*, p. 16.

11.   Rees, T. and Bartlett, W. (1999). Adult guidance services in the European learning society: A Scottish case study. *Studies in the Education of Adults.* vol. 31, p. 23.

12.   Jackson, H. and Haughton, L. (1998). *Adult guidance in community settings, NICEC Briefing.* National Institute for Careers Education and Counselling, p. 2.

13.   The Further Education Funding Council (1997). *Learning Works: Widening Participation in Further Education.* (The Kennedy Report), FEFC.

14.   Edwards, *op. cit.*

15.   Frost, D., Edwards, A. and Reynolds, H. (1995). *Careers Education and Guidance.* Kogan Page; pp. 29–30.

16.   Welsh Office (1999). *Future Skills Wales Project 1998–2007.*

17.   McGivney, V. (1999). *Excluded Men.* NIACE; p. 6.

18.   *Ibid.*, p. 103.

19.   Clayton, *op. cit.*, p. 499.

20.   *Ibid.*, p. 18.

21.   Sargant, *op. cit.*, p. x.

22.   Clayton, *op. cit.*, p. 157.

23.   Sargant, *op. cit.*, p. vii.

6

Stimulating science in rural areas

John R. Nicholson

Introduction

Several strands of rural areas – their economies, communities and environments – conceal a fact that a romantic might wish to deny: science and technology is a core element of rural life and has been for centuries.

East Anglia provides a rich source of examples, some unobtrusive, some blatant, some current and some historical. Dutch expertise, imported in the seventeenth and eighteenth centuries,[1] drained low-level lands for agriculture, dotting the landscape with industrial technology. Windmills, cosy icons of rural Norfolk, wrecked ecosystems for economic gain. Now wind turbines sweep the sky, garnering 'green' energy. The market town of Swaffham has a huge one, providing half the town's electrical power and attracting visitors to Ecotech, a hands-on science centre which is part of Breckland District Council's drive to attract eco-enterprise and tourism into a deprived rural area.

Less dramatic but further reaching is the effect of science on agriculture during the twentieth century. Sophisticated machinery has reduced the need for men and women on the land to the extent that some labourers may work on two or more large farms, each over ten miles apart. Nitrate and phosphate fertilisers multiplied crop production but caused the eutrophication of rivers and broads. The Broads, another reassuring emblem of rural Norfolk, are basically flooded, open-cast pits.[2] Worked for peat, they eventually filled with water, a consequence of thirteenth century climate change[3] and the discovery of a better alternative energy source, coal. Scientists have investigated their change from 'marl lakes' through biologically productive pools to the algae-dominated, less diverse shallows of today. Their research is now being used to reverse this unwelcome trend.[4] The impact of science on rural East Anglia will increase, informing rural conservation, fuelling rural enterprise, stimulating its economy and (potentially) social cohesion. It will also stimulate mistrust and provoke dissent:

> *Science today is exciting, and full of opportunities. Yet public confidence in science has been rocked by BSE; and many people are uneasy about the rapid advance of areas such as biotechnology and IT – even though for everyday purposes they take science and technology for granted. This crisis of confidence is of great importance both to British society and British science.[5]*

The John Innes Centre in Norwich is at the forefront of research on the potential for agriculture and the environment of genetic modification in plants. Lord Melchett's Greenpeace attack on experimental crops in the Norfolk village of Lyng and subsequent acquittal in the Norwich Crown Court has set an unstable stage for twenty-first century debate.[6] Rural communities in Norfolk have had all too little say in the past. A good understanding of the issues – and the science behind the issues – may help them have more of a say (and a more rational say) in their future.

Universities have a vital role in this respect. Research indicates that the public has little confidence in scientists employed by government departments and the media, less even than those employed in the relevant enterprise or by an opposing campaign group. In contrast, the public has considerable confidence in university scientists,[7] presumably perceived as independent and un-allied to the interests of commerce or pressure groups. (This may change as the public discovers more about the funding for scientific research in universities.) If the understanding of science and public debate is to be informed, it is better to be lead by those perceived as neutral – something already understood by Monsanto, if allegations on the company's attempt to load food safety committees with independent scientists have any substance.[8] Arguably, among those most likely to be seen as independent are scientists teaching in continuing education (CE). They could have a vital future role in finding ways to develop a dialogue of trust and mutual respect between 'science experts' and elements of the public (for example, farmers) whose trust in the former has suffered and whose contextual knowledge needs to be acknowledged if society is not, as Wynne warns, to be committed 'to further blind polarisation in the continuous transformations of modernity.'[9]

All this may not have been apparent to those in the Higher Education Funding Council for England (HEFCE) who funded the non-award-bearing (NABCE) projects for 1995–9. Their concerns were focussed on stimulating access and progression in rural areas, as their aims make clear.[10] These were:

- to create new opportunities for access, by provision of NABCE programmes in at least four locations in Norfolk and East Suffolk;
- to support and encourage disadvantaged students from rural areas in progressing to higher education (HE);
- to serve as a focus for other NABCE/access-related developments in targeted locations.

The University of East Anglia (UEA), with its highly-rated science schools, its concern for widening access in rural areas and its successful foundation programme in interdisciplinary science, was well placed to achieve these aims through science. NABCE funding was used to set up a project which still bears the name – the Science Starter Programme (SSP).

Twin challenges: the rural context and attracting adults into science

The SSP was set up in rural areas which, by tradition and a kind of courtesy, fell into that area which the universities of East Anglia, Cambridge and Essex agree to be within the Norwich sphere of influence: essentially the whole of Norfolk and East Suffolk. Two other universities provide significant HE opportunities within the area, Anglia Polytechnic University and the Open University, along with a number of further education (FE) colleges with university affiliations including Suffolk College Ipswich, Otley College and Norwich City College.

The rural elements within this area are diverse. Areas designated as structurally disadvantaged in a European context sit alongside others that are relatively prosperous. Within market towns, villages, and even hamlets such as the one in which I live, this diversity is maintained. (My neighbours include two brothers who eke out a precarious living from a small-holding, a noted surgeon, a newspaper editor, and several council-housed families whose income is low and whose children have not so far experienced HE.)

Popular soft-focus views of restored Suffolk cottages, Poppyland, boating on the Broads, and the bird-life of salt creek, forest and fen can give the outsider – and indeed the insider – a distorted view of rural life in East Anglia. They belie the economic and social disadvantage that is endemic. For many people, life in rural areas can be hard, with low incomes and low expectations. In more than one sense, the East Anglian perspective is one of low horizons. Fifty four per cent of Norfolk lies within the Rural Development Area (RDA) designated by the Rural Development Commission (the UK government agency for economic and social development in rural England), and the third largest RDA in England in terms of population. Part but not all of the RDA includes areas of Norfolk designated under Objective 5b of the European Union's structural funds. Use of these funds was designed to secure the development and adjustment of structurally disadvantaged rural areas. This has been superseded by more general Objective 2 funding aimed at revitalising all areas facing structural difficulties, whether industrial, rural, urban or dependent on fisheries. Those which are not designated as Objective 5 raise the proportion of the county in recognised need of economic and community development to around two-thirds. The picture in rural Suffolk is similar: one of disguised disadvantage in diverse and different communities.

Educational attainment is generally low. In 1991 the percentage of residents over 18, and whose level of highest qualification was a degree or diploma, fell below ten per cent in most of Norfolk's RDA/5b areas,[11] and as low as four per cent in some. Current figures are likely to be higher due to recent efforts by teachers in rural secondary schools and outreach initiatives by Norfolk FE colleges. Wards with both maximum and minimum values were in urban centres. Rural wards were more diverse and some, including Cley and Blakeney on the north coast, had values over 15 per cent. However the same two wards had nearly 40 per cent of its adults over pensionable age – many of whom had moved into the area in their retirement, bringing their qualifications with them and masking the underlying state of affairs within the indigenous community.

Much is said elsewhere in this book about deprivation in rural communities, its causes and its needs, and much of it applies to rural East Anglia. Networking with those who were countering this deprivation proved essential. It enabled the testing and reformulation of my observations and preconceptions, reduced the likelihood of failure, and provided inspiration by imagination and initiative (such as the Workers' Educational Association (WEA)'s Trailblazer Project[12] in Suffolk). Initially I met and consulted with many in the field, including adult education providers in Norfolk; the WEA; colleagues in CE in Norfolk and Suffolk; demographic Planners, Norfolk County Council (NCC); the Economic Development Office (NCC); the Rural Community Council, Norfolk; Community Services, Suffolk County Council; East and West Suffolk community education; science education providers in FE and HE colleges in both counties; and the Open University (which runs its own Into Science course).

As a result, working guidelines were proposed and scrutinised by a steering committee largely drawn from the institutions above. Since then the most productive partners in sustaining effective provision have been Norfolk Adult Education, Trailblazer, The John Innes Research Institute and colleagues in the Universities Association for Continuing Education (UACE) Rural Network.

Attracting adults into science is perceived as a significant problem throughout the UK. The proportion of those entering HE to study sciences has dropped steadily since the 1960s, partly because new opportunities for study have emerged, partly because science-based employment is not regarded as well paid and secure, and partly because science itself is perceived as difficult.[13] Its public image has suffered at the hands of various crises including Chernobyl[14] and the BSE debacle. The Committee for the Public Understanding of Science (COPUS),[15] the British Association for the Advancement of Science, funding agencies like the Biotechnology and Biological Sciences Research Council (BBSRC)[16] and others have tried hard to recoup and promote the public understanding of science in the full knowledge that considerable funding for research comes from the tax-payer.

Much of the activity generated through grants from these bodies has been used to promote science, engineering and technology during Science Week (SET) every March. This initiative, first announced in a White Paper[17] by

William Waldegrave, then Chancellor of the Duchy of Lancaster, is assisted by an annual award from the public purse. Adult Learners Week, organised by NIACE, also affords an opportunity for scientists and science educators to meet with and engage the public. Increasingly non-scientists are making use of the opportunities the SET weeks have provided to reach potential learners in order to stimulate an interest in science which contributes to the university's widening participation programme, or training and employment in local science-based enterprises. Chwarae Teg[18] in Wales, for example, has co-ordinated the co-operation of such diverse groups as Theatr Felinfach (a community radio project), the Arts Council of Wales, Gardd Cymru (the National Botanic Garden of Wales), the National Museum of Wales, the West Wales Craftswomen's Network and Aberystwyth University's physics department.

From its inception, the UEA's SSP adopted a marketing and recruitment strategy that made the following assumptions:

- A significant proportion of the public is intrinsically interested in science and technology according to survey[19] and the popularity of science books[20] and science-based television programmes.[21]
- Many potential adult learners lack confidence, and need guidance and support in making appropriate study and career choices.
- There is no established model for delivering a SSP. Different models would be developed in order to cater for such problems as differences in motivation, travel, cost, child- and parent-care to widen opportunities and to consider their relative effectiveness.

In targeting people in rural areas, the SSP did not focus on or exclude any specific group. It is difficult enough attracting people into science courses without excluding sections of the community such as the apparently comfortably-off, middle class retired person. This would have reduced opportunities for others by reducing numbers below viable thresholds. In any case, creating common ground for different sections of rural communities can in itself be productive.

Strategy and delivery

Four strategies for delivering the programmes emerged. The first was to offer 'tasters' to engage people and make connections. The second was to provide short, issue-based courses and the third to provide opportunities for learning science in non-science contexts – a Trojan Horse approach. Finally the programme provided a substantial core course in the natural sciences, initially unaccredited and later accredited by the Open College Network of North

Anglia. The hope was primarily to engage adults in short, unthreatening experiences of science, to build confidence and interest, and encourage commitment that could lead to enrolment for full- or part-time HE.

Throughout the programme we made use of SET weeks and Adult Learners Week to provide well-publicised opportunities for adults to meet scientists and science educators. This enabled them to discuss career interests, to receive an element of guidance (or book a one-hour guidance session) and to explore avenues for potential development. In its first year the programme ran a mobile hands-on science exhibition, featuring contributions from UEA's science schools, science and engineering in local industries, and primary and secondary schools around Sheringham, Bungay and Thetford. It is significant that in each of these towns enough people were recruited to start a core course of 130 hours. Only in Leiston, Suffolk, where we had hoped to run a course but were unable to exhibit, did we fail to recruit. The titles and occasions for SSP tasters are listed in Table 1.

These events contributed significantly to the promotion and marketing of the programme. The strategy has been to maintain a high profile for the project at local, regional and national level. This has included monthly broadcasts on local radio and occasional press coverage in the national media. Even so, the principal means of recruitment to the programme have been fliers and posters distributed to 'learning shops', libraries, doctors' and vets' surgeries, hairdressers, post offices, colleges and schools. By late 1999, the official end of the venture, the programme had received over 360 requests for information and guidance, with over 100 people taking part in courses of at least 20 hours.

An issues-orientated, twenty-hour course entitled 'You Are What You Eat', dealing with food and genetic engineering was jointly organised with the John Innes Centre. It has run in Bungay and Fakenham, and has stimulated a demand for a related course on food, health and nutrition. Plans to launch two courses, validated by the North Anglia Open College Network at Levels 2 and 3, are being considered along with the provision of copyright-free materials available nationwide.

In 1998, a grant from the Millennium Commission was awarded to fund a programme called START: 'Science and Technology Through Art'. This had to be held by an individual scientist working in tandem with a community institution, in this case the Castle Museum in Norwich. Five- and ten-hour workshops, combining lectures, laboratory work, demonstrations, handling sessions and creative art, were organised at UEA and the Castle Museum for over 120 adults, 45 per cent of whom were motivated enough to find their way into Norwich from distant rural settings. Three related topics were explored: Pigments and Paint, Stained Glass, and Ceramics and Glazes. These were eye-opening for the majority of arts-oriented adults who attended, and indeed the smaller number of adults with a background in the sciences, all of whom enjoyed the experience

Table 1. Awareness-raising/confidence-building event

Event	Date and description	Funding
SET Trail	SET Week March 1996.	COPUS grant, UEA, Norfolk & Waveney TEC
Dyeing to Find Out	Adult Learners Week (ALW) 1996 *Workshops on natural dyes*	SSP Budget
Light Fantastic	Norfolk and Suffolk Shows. *1997 Activities with improvised cameras*	SSP budget
Paint SET	SET97 and ALW 1997. *The art and science of making, testing and using paint*	COPUS grant
Are You Made of the Right Metal?	Norfolk and Suffolk Shows 1997. ALW Fakenham Market, Open day at Otley College, Suffolk. *Extracting iron from cereals, looking at it micro-scopically, discussing related health issues*	SSP Budget
Only Here for the Beer!	SET98 and ALW 1998. *The science of brewing – tastes, tests, talks and quizzes, in conjunction with Woodforde's and Adnams' Ales*	COPUS grant
Something In The Air!	ALW 1999, Norwich Learning Shop. *The science and literature of aromas, perfumes and pongs*	SSP budget

of science and technology in creative contexts. This is arguably how chemistry and other sciences emerged in the first place, as studies of mediaeval art[22] and eighteenth century English porcelain[23] clearly illustrate.

For people ready to commit themselves to a significant period of study, a series of six non-accredited units were developed and taught in three centres in 1996–7. Choices had to be made. What kind of science would succeed with adult learners? What would sustain initial interest, develop self-confidence, and provide a platform for further study? Solomon and Thomas of the Open University approach the science curriculum for adults with these questions:

- What sort of science content should we include?
- What is the appropriate motivation to study science?
- What kind of learning promotes the acquisition of appropriate knowledge?[24]

What did we see as 'appropriate'? Open University students 'have serious learning aims', presumably to acquire a degree and a career in science. In this context a content-lead curriculum is easy to defend. 'Content' in science consists of the facts, concepts and principles of science, the body of knowledge that is science, the kind of science that typically forms the bulk of a university lecture on (say) atomic structure or electromagnetic radiation.

We could not assume that our students' aims, serious as they would be, would be to seek a degree and a career in science – although for some this proved to be the case. We could only assume that there would be a variety of motives in play: fascination perhaps, or Edwards' 'restoration' of education in which adults seek to redress their dropping of science at school for whatever reason – an assumption which was vindicated (see Table 3).[25]

We took a different line in devising our curriculum, working backwards from the order implied by Solomon and Thomas (although that order may not have been their intention). Our questions were more along these lines:

- What kind of learning environment did we want to create?
- What kind of learning would sustain this and promote learning in science?
- What kind of science would motivate learners and develop self-confidence?
- What kind of science would provide a credible foundation for further study?

We wanted an environment that was essentially social, one in which learners felt unthreatened, in which they had views worthy of respect and where they could contribute to the science in hand. We wanted the science to have relevance and to be interesting, reflecting the imaginative use of contexts – an approach employed, for example, in the Open University text *Sensational Chemistry*.[26] We wanted our learners to be active, co-operative, and to enjoy themselves. We wanted their minds and ambitions to be stimulated. We wanted their experience to be fun without being shallow.

From the beginning we decided that process was more important than content, and that content should have context. Harlen made a strong case for using process-based science, maintaining that it 'conveys an image of science as imaginative and created by the human mind … more likely to be seen as interesting and relevant.'[27]

Process-based science has different interpretations but essentially promotes and encourages the acquisition of a set of skills used in investigation; those that scientists use to create their body of knowledge, to test it, to refine it and if

Table 2. The Original Science Starter Core32

Title	Description
The Art of Being Scientific	Acquiring and applying scientific skills and processes in different contexts, with an emphasis on groups defining questions and investigating problems in an open-ended manner; for example, the desirable properties of a post-office elastic band or the pattern of vegetation on a football field.
Energy	A practical look at different forms of energy: their interconversion, efficiency, renewable energy, ways of conserving and measuring it, saving money and feeling good about being 'Green'.
Materials	Exploring the sources, properties and uses of metals, minerals, plastics and composites. Students extracted copper from an ore, dyes from plants, investigated acids and bases, made lime and mortar from chalk and considered the characteristics of chemical change.
Living Systems	Observing and classifying living things and how they function, not only as individual organisms but in partnership or competition. Ecological work focussed on landscape surveys in varied and adjacent habitats.
Models	Exploring and using mental models used to explain important natural phenomena; i.e. the kinetic theory of matter, the atomic model and wave theory.
Global Issues	This element of the course was mapped out by each group according to their interests. Topics have included global warming, acid rain, food and transport

necessary reject parts of it. These include the ability to observe, measure, classify, make predictions and hypotheses, and to design and carry out controlled investigations to test them. It is a foundation for active learning, providing opportunities for discussion, the contribution of ideas, the development of team work and communication skills. A process-orientated curriculum also recognises that learning 'has to take place from within the learner, that ideas which add to useful knowledge cannot be implanted from outside.'[28]

Experience of an earlier UEA initiative indicated that adults respond well to active, investigation-based learning.[29] However, although our Science Starters were often agents in their own learning (and did bring to each session their own experiences, perceptions and capacities for social interaction) the curriculum was not deliberately 'constructivist' as described by Bruner or Driver.[30, 31]

Process, of course, cannot be isolated from content. In science they are interwoven and inseparable. The choice of content was determined by two factors: how appropriate it was to developing a variety of investigation styles and how relevant it was perceived to be to the lives and interests of adults. Table 2 sets out the core curriculum which emerged, one which grew under the influence of the learners interests, experience and demands.

This unaccredited course ran in Sheringham Telecottage, North Walsham Community Centre and the Community Wing at Bungay High school. Bungay is a small market town in North Suffolk, specialising in agriculture, tourism, and printing. The students came with a variety of backgrounds and motives, as Table 3 shows.

Table 3. Profile of students on the core course at Bungay, 1996–7[33]

A	Male, part-time, waged ex-welder, interested in a career researching marine wildlife.
B	Female, un-waged wife and mother, strongly interested in environmental issues.
C	Male, runs small catering business, fascinated by the Discovery Channel and physics.
D	Female, un-waged wife and mother, intends to become occupational therapist.
F	Female, un-waged wife and mother, later accepted for an environmental science degree.
G	Male, retired, part-time business consultant, 'aware of a major gap in his education.'
H	Male, non-degree-holding civil engineer, amateur microscopist, fascinated by sciences.
I	Female, part-time, waged single mother, avid reader of New Scientist, keen to support her daughter's interest in science project work.
J	Female, wife of farmer, had to leave the course due to his illness and run the farm herself.
K	Female, retired English teacher, wanted to reconnect with a childhood 'passion' denied her in her girls' school: i.e. chemistry.

A formative evaluation of this programme by an independent evaluator from UEA showed that participants appreciated their involvement in the development of the curriculum.[34] The chance to 'digress into areas that interested them' with 'everyday connections' within the content was seen as a positive factor. As far as possible, courses were non-hierarchical, structured in such a way as to encourage a 'join at any time' culture. This happened occasionally with, for example, a spinner and weaver joining one group for the section on Materials because it featured plant dyes.

The evaluation also showed that the core course did promote individual success and with it personal confidence and motivation. In its first year, two students decided to progress into the foundation year of UEA's BSc in Natural Sciences and two more to the Open University. It also showed that is possible to use a practical, open-ended, experimental approach within the limitations imposed by working in non-laboratory locations and without much standard science equipment to hand. The facilities afforded by the average kitchen were usually ample. Improvisation using household materials was the norm and encouraged further investigation at home; for example, into the factors determining the browning of freshly-cut apples. In the unit 'The Art of Scientific Investigation' students suggested hypotheses to explain how craters formed on the Moon. They went on to test their impacting meteorite theory using trays of flour sprinkled with cocoa and weighted table tennis balls dropped from different heights (and therefore hitting the surface with known speeds). One student, a man in his 60s with no formal education after the age of 14, devised a way of recording the impacts using slow motion video. Unknown to him at the time, his technique paralleled that of experimental astronomers in the USA who used steel balls fired at rock at near the speed of sound.

Embedding SSP

We wanted to make sure that something worthwhile survived after project funding ceased. As always, that meant finding money. We rejected the notion of seeking further project funding. After four years the SSP had to stand on its own feet. As a non-award-bearing course, the SSP programme could not draw down HE funding so there were two main options open for when the HEFCE grant ran out in 2000. One was to co-operate with further or adult education, to attract FE funding by establishing the appropriate accreditation. The other was to draw down HE funding by developing Level 1 courses as part of a 60-credit Certificate in Science or a 120-credit Certificate in HE in Science. The former strategy had the potential for reaching many people in the rural areas served by adult education and could serve as a feeder for more advanced courses. In the event both strategies were pursued – the FE route during the lifetime of the project and the HE route since then.

In co-operation with Norfolk Adult Education we revised and developed the core course in order to obtain accreditation with the North Anglian Open College Network. The programme, 'Discover New Worlds', was structured and accredited as shown in Table 4.

Table 4. Discover New Worlds

Units	Title & description	Level	Time	OCN Credit
1 & 2	**Discover the World of the Scientist:** Open-ended investigating, relevant to local real-life situations where possible, integrating elements of the major disciplines of biology, chemistry, and physics. Content-free to develop scientific thinking, processes and skills.	1 & 2	20/10 hrs*	1
3 & 4	**Discover the Material World:** Observing, comparing and investigating a range of materials (i.e. metals, building materials, a DIY material (paint), plastics and materials for improved performance) and in so doing, exploring the beginnings of chemistry and how it has affected our lives.	1 & 2	10/5 hrs	0.5
5 & 6	**Discover the World of Energy:** Becoming conversant with the basic science, technology, arguments and issues concerning the generation of different forms of energy for our use. Raising and discussing issues of concern, researching them where necessary, and being aware of local circumstances; e.g. the use of biomass fuels, wind-power and warm mud flats in Norfolk.	1 & 2	10/5 hrs	0.5
7 & 8	**Discover the World Inside You:** Examining ways in which the body works, comparing the life processes found in their own body (e.g. respiration and reproduction) with those in other forms which may or may not be considered as 'living' (e.g. viruses).	1 & 2	10/5 hrs	0.5
9 & 10	**Discover the Outside World:** Modelling the solar system, and building model telescopes to observe it. Exploring smaller systems (e.g. trees, beaches, the edges of a Norfolk Broad or the lawn at home) to explore the interrelationships and complexity linking the physical, climatic and living components of the natural world.	1 & 2	10/5 hrs	0.5
11 & 12	**Discover the World for Yourself:** Undertaking a piece of scientific research, with the emphasis on making use of scientific skills to define a project. Design a suitable investigation, carry it out, evaluate it and report it orally and in written form in the appropriate styles, with references and underlying theory where appropriate. Like units 1 & 2, this unit is process-driven and content-free.	1 & 2	10/5 hrs	0.5

* 20/10 = 20 hours of contact time with the tutor, ten hours of private study

This programme was run successfully by the UEA in Beccles and North Walsham during 1988–99, attracting a total of 26 students. Most gained OCN credit, mainly at Level 2. They also gained one attribute mature students need to progress into HE – the capacity to demonstrate and articulate an informed interest in science.

Successes, failures and reflections

A second, more detailed evaluation of the programme was commissioned in 1998.[35] Essentially summative, this provided independent insight more likely to be objective than an in-house investigation. The evaluation was carried out by questionnaire, aimed at three categories of those who had attended or made enquiries about the programme. These categories, together with response rates, are shown in Table 5

Table 5. Response rates for each category

	A	B	C	
	Attenders	Drop-outs	Inquirers	All
Initial mailing	38	22	155	215
Response rate	26 (68%)	11 (50%)	58 (37%)	95 (44%)

The drop-outs included many who did substantial elements of the core course and could not be regarded as 'drops-outs' in the conventional sense of people not being bothered or motivated. Some were selective in the courses they followed, others found their circumstances changed; for example, because of illness in the family or unforeseen difficulties with transport. The questionnaires addressed several concerns and it is useful to summarise the main findings.

Publicity and marketing made use of free time on BBC Radio Norfolk through a regular monthly science programme to which we contributed. However leaflets in local libraries appeared to be the most widely noticed form of publicity, with 38 per cent and 25 per cent respectively stating that this is how they found out about SSP. The emphasis on no prior qualifications or academic background was highlighted by respondents as contributing to the decision to enquire about the course. Other popular reasons given were a general interest in science, interest in a specific topic, the fun element and the enthusiasm of teaching staff. Reasons for choosing or not choosing to participate in the programme once contact had been made were fairly evenly divided between those with a declared interest in science, and those who were looking for something 'interesting' but were confined to classes in a particular location. Cost, lack of time and unsuitable course timings were the main reasons for not enrolling. Generally, at least 33 per cent of participants found that timing, cost, family commitments and location all contributed to difficulties in attending.

At least 67 per cent of participants in the core programme found the sessions well-taught, very interesting and relevant. For 65 per cent of these, the sessions exceeded expectations. Self-assessment of skill levels in planning investigations, carrying them out and understanding scientific ideas rose substantially. Self-reported levels of confidence also increased. The programme had to compete with others organised by the Open University, Colleges of FE and Cambridge University. Forty per cent of respondents were considering other courses at the time of their SSP enquiry. Firty-two per cent had the eventual aim of gaining further qualifications, with 30 per cent stating they wished to study for a degree. Of those who identified which qualifications they were aiming for, about half of these were science related. The percentage of people aiming for further qualifications was higher amongst those who did not attend any SSP sessions: 70 per cent compared with 44 per cent in group A and 27 per cent in Group B. Clearly non-accreditation of our first course, or the relatively low academic level of the second, was a disadvantage for some people.

All of our first series of courses adopted the traditional teaching and learning mode – meeting regularly in a centre as a group with a tutor. For some this was not possible, so we included questions about learning online. Forty-three per cent expressed an interest this method. Biology headed the list of suggested topics and/or disciplines. It seemed that hardware would not be a major problem for this group, with 75 per cent of those expressing an interest in owning their own computer and three quarters of these possessing a modem. The majority of this group considered they had adequate or good word-processing skills, but poor or non-existent skills in managing email or searching the Internet. Any future developments in learning online would clearly need to address the skills of using the technology effectively.

The profiles of those responding to the questionnaire demonstrates the variety of backgrounds and circumstances in our students referred to earlier in this chapter. Seventy-five per cent were female, mostly between the ages of 26 and 55. Sixty per cent of respondents had children or other care commitments. Forty-five per cent had left school with at least one O-level, four per cent with GCSEs, 26 per cent with A-levels; 20 per cent had a first degree and two per cent a higher degree. Five per cent had left school with no qualifications at all.

Behind these bald statistics and dry conclusions are many human stories of challenge, distress, commitment, disappointment and delight. Many have moved on, confidence enhanced and well motivated. Others have not – one at least deciding that her experience of science was enough to move her well away into other areas!

My own reactions, based on our evaluations and my day-to-day experience, are mixed. On the one hand it was clear that the majority found their experience of learning science to be enriching, enjoyable and confidence-building, helping them to move forward into further study or other learning.

Five are now enrolled on full-time degree courses at UEA, and at least seven on science courses with the Open University. Others sustain their own momentum in two distinct groups. Both are essentially social, both make use of their newly- acquired understanding of science, both are seeking further study and support. The Bungay 'You Are What You Eat' group meets informally over occasional meals in each others' houses to discuss food and genetics respectively. One group in North Walsham is undertaking a short research programme on the recycling of plastics; another a feasibility study of erecting a wind-turbine in the town along the lines of the one in Swaffham – both backed by scientists from the Norwich Research Park with support from a Millennium fund.[36] If a second town turbine turns in North Walsham, the SSP will have made a physical as well as an educational impact.

However the programme has not met the initial aims to the extent I had hoped for. A future wish list would include:

- A higher proportion of younger people, particularly men
- A higher proportion of disadvantaged people with few or no qualifications
- A curriculum which focussed more on rural issues and environments
- A curriculum which responded to a greater degree on students' perceived needs
- A better ways of reaching those in isolated communities or in no community at all.

I would also do more to learn from relevant case studies and research into adult education, particularly in gender-related concerns. The 3:1 female to male ratio of participants seemed to run counter to the received wisdom on female participation in mixed science groups, although in this context I was not surprised. I had taken the possibly simplistic view that adults had a range of interests, motives and needs and that, given the historical and social backdrop to education in East Anglia, these would find expression for more women than men through the SSP. However I did not set out to cater specifically for women.

Subsequent sight of the literature on women in science suggests we were fortunate in our curriculum model, our staffing (more females than males) and the learning style we developed. We certainly did not perceive 'women as a problem', as Barr and Byrke[37] report; more as an integral part of the adult population we were trying to reach and provide for.

My retrospective feeling that the SSP was 'woman-friendly' may of course conceal failure. Those women who applied for and took part in the programme were mostly confident people, well capable of articulating arguments and participating in discussion and debate in the presence of men. I unwittingly neglected women who require 'women-only space', who may have been intimidated by the presence of men as fellow students, tutors or organisers. At that time, I would have rejected women-only courses as patronising, and still feel uncomfortable with the notion. However, there may well be a case for single-sex science provision in rural areas, and not only for women.[38]

Embedding the programme has not succeeded to date. Although the university was able to recruit two groups for the OCN-validated 'Discover New Worlds', Norfolk Adult Education did not recruit enough students to form even one. This was probably due to inadequate marketing and the lack of expert science-related guidance at the Adult Education centres that had hoped to run the programme. Our experience shows that good initial guidance is crucial, with potential students keen to meet their potential tutors, and to see where and how they might learn in future. UEA provided this; Norfolk Adult Education could not.

As the HEFCE-funded element of the programme draws to an end, we are applying lessons learned and looking ahead. The evaluation by Jan Anderson clearly showed the interest in learning science online. Consequently the programme has put resources into a course on Global Warming using the Internet.[39] A pilot study demonstrated its feasibility and provided useful information on how to manage and tutor online. A 10-credit Level 1 course will be available in 2001. Meanwhile a Certificate in Higher Education in science has been running since February 2000. Despite initial set backs we will continue to seek and encourage ways of embedding 'Discover New Worlds' or at least its ethos, in (say) short courses[40] and running new award-bearing courses with two aims in view: to deepen the public understanding of science and to widen participation in HE – in urban as well as rural areas.

This may enable others to respond, as S did recently in a personal letter. S is in her forties, has a disabled husband and two teenage children and lives in a remote riverside hamlet in central Norfolk. In the summer she gardens for a living; in winter there is no work of this kind. She had a thirst for learning, and doubts about her ability. Recently she wrote, following her successful completion of 'Discover New Worlds':

> *I thoroughly enjoyed the classes, thank you, and thank you for restoring my confidence (academical). Lucy may have told you that I am fairly sure of OU funding on the Humanities BA course for 2000, English Lit and hopefully the History of Science and Technology (your inspiration). The maths needed in further science courses would floor me.*

This is not quite the success I had envisaged, but success it is. She is on her way into HE, more aware of her abilities than before, more certain of where she wants to go, and (for good reasons) where she does not. The SSP has helped her to change her life.

Notes

1. Derby, H.C. (1956). *The Drainage of the Fens*. CUP.
2. Green, C. and Hutchinson, J.N. (1960). Archeological evidence. In *The Making of the Broads*. Royal Geographical Society Research Series, no. 3.
3. Lamb, H.H. (1977). *Climate: Present, Past and Future. Vol. 2: Climatic History and the Future*. Methuen.
4. Moss, B. (1983). The Norfolk Broadland experiments in the restoration of a complex wetland. *Biological Review*; vol. 58: pp. 521–61.
5. Select Committee, House of Lords, February 2000, Science and Technology – Third Report, http//www.publications.parliament.uk/pa/ldselect/ldsctech/38/3801.htm.
6. Dawkins, R. 'They were wrong', and Lord Melchett, 'We were right'. *The Observer*, 24 September 2000.
7. Durant, J. and Bauer, M. (1997). *Public Understanding of Science in Britain, Report to the Office of Science and Technology*. COPUS.
8. Barnett, A. 'Monsanto's plan to sway GM debate'. *The Observer*, 24 September 2000.
9. Wynne, B. (1996). May the sheep safely graze? A reflexive view of the expert-lay knowledge divide. In Lash, S., Szerszynski, B. and Wynne, B. *Risk, Modernity and Environment: Towards a New Ecology*. Sage; p. 78.
10. Higher Education Funding Council for England and Wales (1997). Non-Award-Bearing Continuing Education Funded Projects 1995–9.
11. Shaw, M.J. (1991). *1991 Census. A Norfolk Atlas*. Planning and Transportation, Norfolk County Council.
12. Based in Halesworth in Suffolk, a National Lottery-funded Return to Study programme making imaginative use of IT to develop a range of skills in adults from rural communities.
13. Millar, R. (1991). Why is science hard to learn? *Journal of Computer Assisted Learning*; vol. 7, no. 2: pp. 66–74.
14. Wynne, B. (1990). Misunderstood misunderstandings; social identities and public understanding of science. In *Misunderstanding Science? The Public Reconstruction of Science and Technology*. CUP; pp. 19–46.
15. Committee for the Public Understanding of Science, The Royal Society.
16. Biotechnology and Biological Sciences Research Council.
17. Announced at the Annual Meeting of the British Association for the Advancement of Science, 1993.
18. Chwarae Teg is the Welsh wing of Fairplay (Workforce) Ltd., a group dedicated to encouraging and supporting women into work.
19. Durant, J., Evans, G. and Thomas, G. *Nature*, 340, July 1989.

20. Rodgers, G. (1992). The Hawking phenomenon. *Public Understanding of Science*; vol 1, no. 2: pp. 231–234.
21. Waldegrave (1993) in his White Paper quotes John Birt's figures of 4.7m viewers for *Tomorrow's World*, 5.9m for *QED*, and 1.9m for *Horizon* set against 0.4m for the arts programme, *The Late Show*.
22. Cennino Cennini (1330). *Il Libro del Arte*, available in translation from Penguin.
23. Reilly, R. (1992). *Josiah Wedgewood*. Macmillan.
24. Solomon, J. and Thomas, J. (1997). Science education for the public understanding of science. *Studies in Science Education*; vol. 33: pp. 61–90.
25. Edwards, R. (1997). *Changing Places*, Routledge.
26. Bennett, S. *et al*. (1995). *Our Chemical Environment*. Book 4 of ST240, Open University.
27. Harlen, W. (1989). Education for equal opportunities in a scientifically literate society. *International Journal of Science Education*; vol. 11, no. 2: pp. 125–34.
28. Harlen, W. (1993). Education for equal opportunities in a scientifically literate society. In Whitelegg, E., Thomas, J. and Tresman, S. eds. *Challenges and Opportunities for Science Education*. The Open University.
29. *Why Should Kids Have All The Fun?* An outreach programme organised and evaluated internally by Imelda Race of the School of Chemical Sciences, UEA, 1993–4.
30 Bruner, J.S. (1986). *Actual Minds, Possible Worlds*. Harvard University Press.
31. Driver, R. and Oldham, V. (1986). A constructivist approach to curriculum development in science. *Studies in Science Education*; vol. 13: pp. 105–22.
32. Note the course was not assessed or accredited, although many individuals completed assignments set at their request, and a portfolio of their work. Even those that did not expressed a sense of achievement. Extra field trips and visits to UEA for a seminar on progression and a tour of science departments added 12 hours to the core time of 120 hours.
33. A and F were accepted on UEA's Foundation course for natural sciences, D will one day achieve her ambition, I is considering our Certificate HE course in science, and K could get an excellent degree in chemistry should she ever choose to.
34. Race, I. (1997). *Science Starter Programme Evaluation Report 1997*. An interim formative evaluation by individual and group interviews and by questionnaire, UEA.
35. Anderson, J. (1998). *Evaluation of the Science Starter Programme 1996–1998*. Economic Research Centre, School of Economics and Social Studies, UEA.
36. A consortium including UEA, the John Innes Centre and The Institute of Food Research.
37. Barr, J. and Birke, L. (1998). *Common Science? Women, Knowledge and Science*. Indiana University Press.

38. Teaching in high school I have seen a few boys retreat, blunt, inarticulate and sometimes resentful in the face of feminine achievement in the lab. I had no sympathy with them at the time, but wonder now if they are part of another self-denied minority who may well by now deserve some attention.

39. Example pages from the course can be seen at http//www. uea.ac.uk/fdl/gwarming.

40. A former Science Starter and GMB Training and Development Officer asked me to design and deliver a one-day course for Norfolk schools' dinner ladies. She asked me to use the approach she had experienced through Science Starter. She had enjoyed it, we used it, and it worked well according to the 17 women and one man who took part.

7

Learning Within Reach

Roseanne Benn

Introduction

In 1994 the Higher Education Funding Council for England (HEFCE) issued a circular which stated that the only continuing education (CE) provision which would receive formula funding was that which could contribute to the student gaining a university award.[1] This was to have a major impact on the provision of most CE departments at pre-1992 universities in England and Wales by resulting in the credit rating of most CE provision within two to three years. Though there were positive outcomes to this mainstreaming of CE work, particularly in terms of increased progression for students, an unwelcome consequence was a reduction in both the number of courses and venues offered. At the University of Exeter it was felt that this, rather than accreditation *per se*, had the effect of excluding many potential students.

Other factors were also affecting the south-west peninsula. It suffers from the various educational problem linked to rurality. A substantial sector of the population in Devon and Cornwall lives in small towns and villages. This distributed settlement pattern and the decline of public transport have led to a range of disadvantages affecting people in rural areas whose access to many facilities, including education, is restricted. Travel is expensive, time-consuming and, for those who cannot afford their own transport, often not possible at all. While potential learners in urban areas are more able to make good use of educational opportunities, those resident in rural areas have been disadvantaged by geographical factors, often aggravated by low incomes. This can affect all rural dwellers to a greater or lesser extent, but economic restrictions tend to limit educational opportunities particularly for women and for the elderly. Many families and retired people have low disposable incomes. The south-west peninsular has the highest proportion of elderly people in the UK and many of them live in rural areas. The majority of older people are women. Demographic changes in the south west, such as longer life expectancy and the influx of older people from climatically less favoured parts of the country, are increasing the numbers of 'third agers'. Many retire to the

105

south west for the beauty and peace of the countryside and the perception of a better quality of life.

The Department of Continuing and Adult Education (DCAE) at the University of Exeter searched for ways of tackling the two problems of rurality (in the specific context of the south west) and changes in funding. At the same time, HEFCE, looking to counteract some of the disadvantages of the circular mentioned above, established a Widening Provision Initiative in 1995. The DCAE applied for money for a distance learning project that would take higher education (HE) out to rural communities and hence, by complementing its face-to-face provision, attempt to overcome the identified problems.

It was hoped that the new opportunities for learning offered by the combination of information technology (IT) and telecommunications would provide access possibilities for learners in remote areas with poor transport. Over an extended period, such learning could build a basis for social benefits, derived from a wider skill base. It could also lead to enhanced employment opportunities and certainly enrich the life of individuals and their communities. The project, it was hoped, could also contribute to the economic regeneration of outlying areas by raising expertise in the use of new technologies.

The Learning Within Reach project

Having identified distance as a central problem, the DCAE was successful in its application for funding for four years to support affordable provision for rural students who could not reach existing programmes of study. This project became known as Learning Within Reach (LWR). The project's planned outcomes were identified as follows:

- A model of teaching through modern technology;
- A programme of initial and ongoing staff development for full-time and part-time tutors;
- A programme of courses to train students in the essentials of using IT for distance learning, such as initial IT awareness packs, with additional backup information, designed also to provide extra support for students working from home using the existing successful university publication, *Home Alone: A Guide to Independent Study*;[2]
- A range of designed, piloted and implemented, award-bearing courses for independent distance learning, supported by a library of information packs in appropriate formats for each course;
- Identification of appropriate hardware and software to support the work of DCAE staff and of students working from home, as well as identification of services and support for the hardware;
- Identification of suitable locations for community access to hardware and agreements with institutional partners on location of and access to hardware;

- Use and development of research into learning in the third age and into distance learning by adults;
- A quarter of the university's mainstream CE assisted by the developments from the project.

Within the time constraints of the project, pragmatic aspects for course implementation were defined and given priority. For the project team, these were converted into the following questions:[3]

- What are the appropriate technologies for distance learning?:
  - which technologies could be introduced immediately for the initial pilot courses?
  - which technologies may become practicable during the later part of the project?
- How can students gain access to equipment for course delivery and support and acquire the requisite skills?
- How can the cost for using the above technology be kept low for students?
- How can we gather and balance the necessary breadth of expertise (involving academics, the library and its staff) to provide high-quality courses?
- What are the staff involvement and development issues in the provision of computer-based or supported distance courses?
- Can we balance the needs of distance students for adequate support with the need for departments to make courses financially viable in the medium and long term?
- How can we incorporate this initiative into existing departmental provision and future plans?

Developing Learning Within Reach

It was essential that LWR provision should be integrated closely with DCAE's face-to-face provision. A strategic review of the DCAE work resulted in the identification of eight major subject areas (archaeology/Egyptology, counselling, environmental studies, historical studies, humanities, languages, literary studies, and theology) and the reorganisation of all DCAE's work into these areas. The LWR provision was located in this framework. This ensured coherence in subject provision and appropriate quality-assurance arrangements. In the early stages of the project, staff development money was concentrated on improving staff knowledge and expertise in distance delivery. This was achieved by offering only those courses that were well established in more conventional mode. With the growth in confidence, programmes are now being designed and offered in distance-learning mode only where it is thought that there would not be sufficient recruitment for a face-to-face class – or, indeed, where this is now the lecturer's preferred mode of delivery.

The project concentrates on the lifelong learning needs of the rural communities in Cornwall, Devon, West Somerset and West Dorset. The numbers of potential participants may be considerable, but their awareness of new and computer-based approaches to distance learning is only beginning to develop. This raising of awareness has been helped by the national interest in, for example, lifelong learning, learning societies, learning cities and learning partnerships. Publicity is through normal channels but in addition there has been media interest leading to newspaper articles and radio appearances. Project money has allowed new approaches, such as flyers in freebie newspapers, to be tried, but with limited success. As always in adult education, word of mouth is a major source of recruitment. Channels such as the University of the Third Age (U3A), whilst supportive in principle, have not been especially significant for recruitment. Full publicity is available on the Internet but it is not yet clear how effective such publicity has been. It is likely that this will gain importance as a means of recruitment.

The LWR programme consists of a number of accredited courses, underpinned by a series of study tutorials and non-accredited, 'taster' short courses to support the study. It will eventually be possible to build up credit gained towards university awards of certificates, diplomas and degrees. A range of IT courses, only available through LWR, is being developed.

Staff development

In the early stages of the project, staff development focused on training days. Typically they offered presentations and workshops on IT; familiarising staff with the use of the Internet and its facilities for electronic access to the library and various forms of distance learning, and general library issues. However, as the project developed it became clear that the most useful form of staff development was through discussion with the project officer. A considerable proportion of his time is now spent on this 'informal' staff development.

A learning resource centre was established containing a wide range of useful material.[4] This includes the development of a web-based resource for tutors on all aspects of the project and is available on the DCAE server. This provides a considerable amount of information, either directly or though offering access to linked websites, online papers and news groups, LWR news, distance courses and conference information. Like all web-based materials, this resource can be easily updated as additional information and materials become available. Even a cursory inspection of this interactive resource reveals an impressive amount of information which has been collated for easy access by DCAE course tutors. The results and experience of both tutors and students is being disseminated within the university through its distributed learning network.

ICT issues

The delivery of learning material and tutor support is via the Internet, or the more traditional method of post and telephone, or a combination of both. Use of the Internet is being encouraged as a method for providing teaching and learning material and for communication. Discussion pages and bulletin boards on the website enables the creation of a 'virtual classroom' that can help to reduce the sense of isolation often felt by students studying at home. Telephone and postal services are used to support those who are unable to access a computer or choose not to – although these students miss out on some of the opportunities for 'class' discussions and other web-based resources.

Students are supported in their use of IT through a range of starter tutorial packs. These provide an introduction to some basic software packages (word processing, spreadsheets, email and web browsers). Students are able to register with the university IT services and have password access to dial into the university network if they wish. They are also provided with information on other Internet connection options.

Students who do not own their own computers are directed to facilities near to where they live. These might be an open-access centre, public library or a Rural Area Training Information Opportunities (RATIO) centre of which there are now 35 in the south west. In the latter, students can get computer training and support, access to the course materials on the Internet and communicate by email. Such centres frequently have video links that may contribute to the use of video conferencing in the future.

Access to computers is seen as an integral (though not essential) part of distance learning. Most computers are capable of providing for the more basic requirements, such as word processing and email. However, computers need to be reasonably powerful if electronic work files are to be passed from student to tutor and back; reading materials are to be ready formatted; lists, tables and spreadsheets are to be used; and software required to make full access to the extensive facilities of the Internet. The cost for this, and for the associated hardware, can be avoided if students have easy access to computers in an existing IT centre. For students who want to buy their own machines, PC Pentiums are seen as standard. A computer would also require a modem to access email or an appropriate card for an Internet connection, as well as a printer – in all, a very considerable expense.

To ensure file compatibility for tutors and students, there has to be agreement on the type of operating system and software for common use. (Cross-platform compatibility is not easy to handle.) The common software for the project is Microsoft Office, used for word processing, spreadsheets and presentation.

To put learning within reach for the remote learner, it is imperative that information sources are defined for each course and that access to a whole body of information sources is a practical reality for each student. Some of these sources are already available. The university library offers direct links to students (and staff) using computers, so that they can browse remotely, select from available paper sources and order books. LWR students can acquire the requisite skills through one of their introductory electronic tutorials. Other materials can be located independently by students through the use of search engines. Here, however, lies a problem: not all students have computers available – and even when they do, the platform and software they are using may not be suited to the particular format in which the information is offered. In addition, some learners (and some tutors) may require a substantial amount of initial support. For this reason, paper-based support materials and more familiar technologies are still used by about half the students.

Course tutors recommend appropriate sources of information, which vary with course requirements. For distance learning, accessibility of resources has to be taken into consideration. These considerations are included in course development procedures, and their selection will ultimately depend on the course requirements and the decisions made by individual course tutors. While traditional paper-based sources, such as journals and books, will continue to be used in many instances, some tutors prepare their own materials for electronic distribution. To an increasing extent, the Internet will gain importance for students. Initially, distance students can use its facilities for accessing the university library services, for bibliographic information or for ordering specified books. The Internet also offers a nearly unlimited range of information sources for browsing and downloading. LWR offers dedicated pages on the Internet to support educators and students alike.

Non-accredited courses and study materials

Although DCAE is concentrating on the teaching of credit-rated programmes, there is a rationale for offering a limited non-accredited programme. To optimise the use of student and tutor time, distance students require a high level of support. The DCAE is trying to address the problem though the provision of support materials which could be described appropriately as pre-course learning. These non-accredited courses and materials can be grouped as follows:

1. To support the development of study skills, DCAE provides an independent study guide which is relevant for all students and offers advice to distance learners.[5] Topics range from preparation to study, though thinking skills, gathering and processing information to writing and research. Examination techniques including revision are included.

2. A range of computer skills is covered by short tutorials, which are designed to fit the needs of distance students. These tutorials are provided in electronic format, with the introductory modules also in paper version. They are provided either as individual skills or as a complete pack through DCAE or local centres, at a cost of £30 for the set or at £5 per module.

Their use is optional, but highly recommended for those
requiring support. They cover the following skills that may be
needed for distance learning:
- Introduction to the use of the mouse and the keyboard of
  a computer;
- Understanding and using your PC;
- Getting online: understanding and using the University
  of Exeter Network;
- Using WORD to present your work;
- Using EXEL spreadsheets for tables, graphs, simple
  calculations and statistics;
- Using Exeter University Library and the Worldwide Web
  to access information.

3. A range of non-accredited foundation courses, covering
   literature, history, archaeology and environmental studies is
   provided. Students who take part in the LWR programme study
   within the existing modular course framework offered by
   DCAE. However, the courses are adapted to meet their study
   needs and a substantial amount of specific support is provided
   by the course tutors and the project officer through a variety of
   pathways which will be selected to match requirements and
   constraints at any given time. Programme provision is
   integrated to allow for mixed-mode study.

Partnerships

Partnerships were initially seen as crucial for the successful implementation
of this project. Two links were especially important; RATIO, in order to
ensure all students had access to local ICT facilities, and U3A for its third age
membership.

RATIO is a European-funded project set up to promote economic activities
in areas which have suffered from socio-economic exclusion through
geographical remoteness and/or industrial decline. The rural and post-
industrial areas of the south west fall into this category. The project's remit is
the creation of a visible telematics infrastructure, at local level, to attract a
range of local information and training providers and encourage dialogue
between them and their clients. Its ultimate aim is to meet the training needs
of local people and create the basis of a skilled work force for the support and
development of small- and medium-sized enterprices (SMEs) in the region.
The project is based at the Plymouth College of Further Education. RATIO
comprises a total of 35 centres, with IT facilities, providing email, Internet
links and video conferencing to deliver business, vocational and training
information and services to local communities across the south west. The aim
of this network of local innovation centres is to bring modern technology to
remote rural areas, at a modest cost to the individual user.

RATIO agreed to offer their facilities to DCAE's LWR students for a small fee. These included email and access to the Internet without a set time limit (although there were some practical restrictions, such as booking times). Advice for users and updated information is available on the RATIO website. Both the award-bearing and non-award-bearing courses of this programme can be delivered through the use of the RATIO facilities. Collaboration with RATIO to utilise video conferencing for course delivery is a future possibility. RATIO is installing PictureTel for those centres that provide ISDN lines, and Creative Share Vision PC3000 that will work with analogue telephone lines. Leaflets about LWR courses are available through RATIO centres.

The project was given excellent access to RATIO centres due to the motivation and enthusiasm of one of the RATIO development officers. However, student participation was limited. About a half preferred the postal mode whilst many others already owned their own computers. It will be interesting to see if this option is used more in the future, as both LWR and RATIO become better established.

The U3A national group seemed an ideal vehicle for contacting the third-age target group. This is a voluntary organisation for retired, or semi-retired, people from all walks of life, generally from their mid-50s upwards. Members meet like-minded people to expand their knowledge, share interests or acquire new skills. There is a London-based office for a U3A association, representing local U3A groups. However, the membership fee is relatively high, and a substantial number of local groups – including several of the Devon groups – have chosen not to be associated. Consequently, it was difficult to keep in close contact with these dispersed groups. Nonetheless, LWR provides attractive study facilities for older learners, particularly those in remote areas. Local U3A organisations offered to provide channels of information about courses and facilities. There is regular communication with local groups and dissemination of LWR publicity materials. To date, it is not clear how much recruitment comes from this source.

The students

The first courses ran in 1998–9, with over 90 students enrolled on 11 courses. Students ranged in age from 18 to 78 years. The average age was 46. However almost half were under 34. Fifty per cent had had no previous experience of HE. They included single parents, people in full- and part-time employment, unemployed, pensioners and individuals with disabilities and mental health problems. A number of students had disabilities that made access to face-to-face classes impossible; others were full-time carers of relatives or children. The gender ratio was approximately one-third male to two-thirds female. About one half lived in rural areas or villages. All wanted the courses to carry credit-rating and were aiming for progression to higher levels of education. All stated that distance learning suited their needs.

Enrolment has increased rapidly to over 1,000 students in 2001–2. There is a clear demand from students for accredited provision and pressure on DCAE to provide sufficient courses by this mode for students to obtain the full range of awards on offer to face-to-face students.

Outcomes and reflections on the project

An independent evaluation of the project by Hedda McShea shows that the target outcomes, listed at the beginning of this chapter, were achieved. A model of teaching has been developed which appears to keep student retention high and fulfil quality-assurance criteria. However, the financial situation is still not fully resolved. A programme of staff development has been set in place, which seems to meet both full- and part-time tutor needs. The IT and study-skills programmes are now both established and running well. A growing proportion of the university's mainstream award-bearing, part-time programme is offered via distributed learning, supported by a library of information packs. Appropriate hardware and software has been selected for the LWR programme. The RATIO centres have been identified as suitable locations for community access to hardware and agreements have been negotiated to allow access.

The project has benefited from existing research into learning in the third age and distance learning by adults. It is hoped that, through publications such as this, it will itself contribute to the body of knowledge in this area of lifelong learning. Within the university, the programme is regarded as successful, innovative and contributory to university-wide initiatives. It is now well established within the Department's provision and is proving popular with students. It not only attracts students from the target groups but also those with needs that are not met by conventional face-to-face provision.

However there are problems. Some of these are financial. During the life span of the project, financial support was provided for course development and support, as well as for the ongoing training of lecturers and tutors. In addition, there was funding for project staff and for equipment. Once this project ceased, money had to be found from additional mainstream funding under an aspect of the Funding Council's Widening Participation Initiative. The DCAE has struggled to keep the cost to the student at face-to-face levels but has had to charge a small premium.

It has also taken far longer than originally envisaged to proceed through all the various stages in implementing many aspects of the courses. Planning and uploading onto the website is time-intensive. This is also true for the provision of student and tutor support. Creating distance-learning materials and courses and supporting them properly is not a quick or cheap option. It has been necessary to take small steps and not place too much emphasis on the technology. The majority of students using the website as part of the course are new to computers and the Internet. Therefore, time is better spent keeping the technology simple, adding more as students become more confident and the technology becomes more user-friendly. In addition, there are administrative problems such as fitting a new 'style' of student into the existing system. The small project team is very stretched in supporting a wide range of tutor and student IT abilities.

Copyright for online publication of study material and images is another major problem. Whilst advice has been received from the university librarian and has been drawn to the attention of all course tutors, there remain difficult areas, such as the provision of links to websites for students. The responsibility for breach of copyright lies with the provider of such links and this will require ongoing monitoring. A related serious and substantial problem is around providing access to library and study resources for distance learners. Marketing within a large rural region is slow and expensive. Spreading the message throughout the south west that there are new and accessible opportunities for studying at home provided by the University of Exeter takes time and money. Quality issues are as, if not more, important for LWR courses than for face-to-face. Ensuring standards are maintained is particularly time-consuming.

It was anticipated that the main interest in LWR would come from the rural communities. In fact the programme has attracted a diverse group of people, some of whom are housebound (including those with physical disabilities and agoraphobia), carers or people who work difficult hours. There are also third-agers including people retiring or who have retired to the south west. Only approximately one half of the first intake came from rural areas, despite the targeted publicity. In order to ensure sustainability, the programme was offered with the same concessionary rates as the face-to-face provision although, publicity emphasised the saving in transport costs. However, it is arguable that the programme is no more affordable to the economically disadvantaged than our face-to-face provision. These outcomes suggest that removing the need to travel to classes with set programme times attracts a wide and variable group of students. They also indicate that the rural issue is more complex than just problems of distance. It may be that considerable work needs to be done outside the scope of this project to change attitudes, aspirations and expectations.

There are pedagogic issues in adapting a variety of teaching styles and subjects to online distance learning. Students also have had to cope with a steep learning curve: wrestling with IT as new users; insecurity about participating in an online environment; insecurity around participating in study programmes at HE level; learning to study independently; and accessing course reading materials. The only factor that affects all potential students under the LWR project is the problem of access to learning. Some students may be familiar with accessing electronic information, but others require introductory support during the early phase of their studies. Similarly, some require basic study skills, but not all. However, most require some study-skill support. Those who are new to academic study need considerable support during the early stages of their studies. This is, in effect, a compounded disadvantage for this group.

Those who already have effective study skills can utilise new methods of using electronic information and thus enrich their studies though communication with course leaders and members of their peer group. However capable and experienced any student might be, a major requirement for those involved in distance study is communication – ensuring that students can access their tutors for feedback on their progress and benefit from constructive discussion. Communication between students, to encourage peer-group cohesion and support, is another major factor in successful distance learning. Yet again it appears that the iron rule of education is in operation. The already advantaged, skilled and articulate are likely to gain most from LWR.

Most courses offered under LWR are also offered face-to-face. If face-to-face courses do not enrol sufficient numbers in some locations, then the LWR mode is offered to prospective students instead. This leads to less disappointment for enthusiastic and motivated students, but these students may well not be from the target groups. This use of LWR helps to increase, but not necessarily widen, participation. It is decisions such as this that tend to distort and counteract the original targeting. In this project, as in many others, it is difficult to restrict or even focus targeting on specific groups.

Conclusions

This project has been demanding and at the same time rewarding. It does seem that providing distance learning opportunities is an effective way of widening access to HE. It also makes the University of Exeter's CE provision available, not only to those who were excluded by centralisation resulting from the funding changes, but also to a new and wider group of learners. There have been other spin-offs. Course tutors who support both face-to-face students and distance learners can use the creation of web-based materials as an additional resource for the former group. This benefits both tutors and students. However, it requires considerable time, effort and resources to develop materials for courses to be delivered in this way and for tutors and students to adapt to a new way of working. Parallel with this is the cost and effort of informing the public of the opportunities provided through this route. The most obvious lesson to date is that this work takes time to implement and time to mature into an effective provision of lifelong learning and widening participation.

In many ways the issues raised are common to all HE institutions (HEIs) that have to deploy resources to communities located at considerable distances from their main sites. They need to assess the cost/benefit ratio of engaging in activities with small communities. At present an examination of geodemographic mapping shows that staff from HEIs have to travel considerable distances to work with disadvantaged communities in the south west. Since population densities in many parts of the region are low, many settlements have very small individual populations. HEIs have therefore tended to focus their attention on larger communities since these have the greatest chance of providing 'viable' student numbers. The LWR programme is beginning to counteract this tendency by providing a wide range of part-time learning opportunities to the rural south west. Nevertheless this form of study, can be very demanding for those returning to study, especially when opportunities to attend face-to-face for occasional study days are constrained by distance.

Although some initiatives like the south west's RATIO centres have been located in smaller settlements, often individuals from the most isolated and disadvantaged communities still have to travel to access learning opportunities. Unfortunately if there is no public transport (as is likely) and no access to a car, this apparently short travelling distance is equally as disempowering as a 50- or 100-mile journey. This illustrates the need to continue to make provision through paper-based study materials.

There is no doubt that the topographical and geographical configuration of the south-west region does have an effect on individuals' ability to access HE provision. The dispersed nature of many rural populations means that HEIs have more difficulty in resourcing their contribution to community development and regeneration. This project has again illustrated the complexity of rural deprivation. Where individuals have come from a privileged or relatively privileged background, they are able to enjoy the tranquillity of the countryside and may take full advantage of initiatives such as LWR. However, for those people living in rural areas who come from educationally and socially deprived backgrounds (as is common in much of rural Cornwall, Devon, Dorset and Somerset), accessing HE requires more than just a change in mode of study. It requires raised aspirations and increased accessibility, in the fullest sense, before the HE provision that so many of us take for granted is truly available to them.

Nonetheless, although distributed learning is still beleaguered by problems, the LWR project has made a real contribution to widening participation to HE provision and to the goal of social inclusion. Like so many such projects, it has made HE available to a wider group – wider also than the original target group. The outcome is arguably none the worse for that.

Acknowledgements

The author is indebted to the reports of the two Project Development Officers, Caroline Whiting (1995–7) and Michael Jeffries-Harris (1997–), and the project evaluation of Hedda McShea. The success of the project is due to their hard work.

Notes

1. Higher Education Funding Council for England (1994). Circular 3/94, HEFCE.
2. Benn, R. and Douglas-Dunbar, A. (1994). *Home Alone: A Guide to Independent Study.* Independent Study Unit, University of Exeter.
3. Whiting, C. (1998). Widening access: a curriculum for distance learning. In Benn, R. and Fieldhouse, R. eds. *A Critical Assessment of Adult Continuing Education Curriculum Development in Practice.* Occasional Paper 3, University of Exeter, Centre for Research in Continuing Education; pp. 29–35.
4. Such as Field, J. ed. (1997). *Electronic Pathways.* NIACE (technical manuals; distributed learning journals; and other relevant literature).
5. Benn and Douglas-Dunbar , *op. cit.*

8

Rural Broadnet and the electronic village hall
Len Graham and John O'Donoghue

Introduction

Rural Broadnet, a University of Wolverhampton rural information technology (IT) project, was established in order to address and overcome the problems of isolation and poor public transport which limit access to further and higher education (FE and HE) in rural areas. Working with local communities, groups and agencies, the project helped to establish a number of rural information and communications technology (ICT) resource centres and to facilitate the delivery of a range of education courses for local people. The work of Rural Broadnet also became involved with rural economic regeneration through contacts with small- and medium-sized enterprises (SMEs) and self-employed people for whom training and education needs could be met through local and flexible delivery.

Locality and the project

Wolverhampton borders considerable expanses of rural countryside to the west, south and north . The chosen area of operation, Shropshire, is a large county stretching west to the border with Wales. It was within this westerly border area, the Marches, that the project focussed its work. Shropshire is predominantly rural and much of the south and west is rolling hill country. The population spread in the south west is at half the national average density and is amongst the lowest in the country. Population decline, evident over much of this century, has more recently reversed so that there is now a net increase in population in rural areas. A significant proportion of incomers are middle-aged, middle-class resource importers, while many of the leavers are the young and unskilled. Local authority boundary changes have meant that the Wolverhampton University campus in Telford, originally a Shropshire campus, is now located in the separate local authority of Telford and Wrekin. There are FE colleges in Telford and the four, widely-spread Shropshire market towns – Oswestry, Bridgnorth, Ludlow and Shrewsbury.

The impact of social, economic and technological change and the consequent process of long-term agricultural decline, allied to the major food crises of recent decades (such as salmonella and BSE) followed by reform of the Common Agricultural Policy, has created the most severe problems for farmers operating in marginal areas such as the Marches. Much local employment was related to agriculture and most companies were at the lower end of the SME scale, with the majority being sole traders. The 1996 Wolverhampton Business School study of local business in the area indicated low skill levels (including IT) among the local work force and low participation rates in training.[1] Figures for 1997 from Shropshire Chamber's Household Survey showed a ten per cent drop in numbers trained within the Shropshire workforce and also indicated that less than half the workforce in Shropshire consider themselves well qualified in IT.[2] There were generally low participation rates in 16-plus education and a high level of out-migration of this age group. Although agricultural decline had meant that Shropshire qualified for European Union 5b status, which offered grants for economic regeneration, in the western border areas, economic development initiatives had to compete with superior funding available in close-by Wales.

Rural Broadnet was project-funded by the Higher Education Funding Council for four years from 1995–9 under the widening participation programme, with a mandate to provide non-award-bearing courses. Its objectives included the establishment of two electronic village halls within its first year, and the facilitation of education and training delivery to local rural areas. The brief was to utilise IT to overcome the barriers – particularly of distance and isolation – faced by rural communities in accessing education, training and associated advice, guidance and information.

Target groups included women returners, older people, the 16–25 age group, those on low incomes and small businesses, particularly farming, with little tradition of in-service training.

Methodology drew both from community development and andragogy. From the former, great emphasis was laid on locally-identified needs, active local self-help and the establishment of working partnerships between local communities and other agencies. From the latter were taken the ideas of Malcolm Knowles: that adult learners can, with support, identify their own learning needs and can become motivated and self-directed.[3] It was also recognised that adult learners throughout their lives have an increasing need to undertake learning episodes, continuing professional development, particularly where these contribute to current life and career needs.

In addition to the target groups and the project's continuing education (CE) focus, it became clear that issues of economic regeneration would need to be addressed. These were from any perspective integral to the learning needs of local communities and to their continued vitality and viability. As the crisis in agriculture deepened through the late 1990s, economic regeneration became an even more pressing issue. Government and local regeneration agencies increasingly identified the significance of IT for economic regeneration and the potential of telematics for 'e-business' applications in rural areas. IT was clearly identified as an important education and training need for local businesses and communities. Additionally, it was recognised that failure to address low skills in IT would lead to further economic decline and to a widening of the gap between the technological 'haves' and 'have-nots'.

When? Where? How? Why?

The importance of economic regeneration was immediately emphasised in the first phase of the project. This entailed working with local communities to plan and organise the development of the two electronic village halls, which would be local IT centres with training and education functions. The two centres developed differently, but in each case local representatives identified economic regeneration as a primary need and objective.

The Vron IT centre was situated in the newly-built community centre at Newcastle-on-Clun, a hamlet of 133 people remotely located near the Welsh border and a centre for surrounding settlements. In addition to the community centre, it also has a primary school, post office, church and pub, and three buses per week to different destinations – although none to the nearest community education provider. The community centre was built to replace a run-down village hall. Local people decided to include an IT centre in order to increase work opportunities by providing local IT training and creating a Teleworking Enterprise. The community centre houses a pre-school children's centre, a meeting hall, youth room, bar and social area and is used by many local groups.

Arising from the teleworking proposal, local training needs were immediately identified and Rural Broadnet was requested to facilitate basic IT and teleworking training for a small group of workers. The Vron IT centre was equipped with five networked Pentium computers and a printer, provided on loan and installed by Wolverhampton University. An Internet connection via a modem was installed, but upgraded to ISDN2 communications in order to facilitate training. In its first year, the Vron centre ran entirely on volunteer support but from the second year secured funding to employ staff to manage the centre. The community centre has a management committee of local people.

The Bishops Castle IT resource centre was developed by the local Rural Challenge regeneration programme, with support from South Shropshire District Council and other local agencies. Housed in a large converted factory, it also included offices for local agencies and businesses and six small business workshops. The dual function of the centre was to provide IT access for the local community and also to provide IT support to the businesses housed within the project, and to SMEs within the rural area to boost economic regeneration. Staffing of two full-time and two part-time posts includes the manager and caretaker who have responsibilities for another project. Bishop's Castle is a small market town close to the Welsh border with a population of 1,570. It serves as a local centre for a large, sparsely-populated and hilly rural hinterland

and the town's facilities are used by some 9,000 people. The IT centre has ten Pentium computers, networked with server and printers. There are also colour and black photocopiers, a scanner, two Internet connections, with ISDN2 communications, fax and other minor equipment. The management committee consists of representatives from the local council and other local agencies.

The activity

Both IT centres function so that computers may be booked on a drop-in or hire basis. Both run a range of training courses, from introductory courses for people without IT skills through to courses on specific software programmes, or targeted at specific groups such as women and small businesses. The bulk of their training has been conducted through traditional pedagogy, using face-to-face tutors, with a small amount of self-directed work supported by paper packs, disks or CD programmes. In the opening phase of their development, Rural Broadnet gave direct support to the training of staff and users within the centres. A priority was to bring users into the centres. Those members of the community with no IT skills were targeted and training groups were rapidly filled with enthusiastic students. Rural Broadnet also identified and supplied suitable CD and paper-based learning materials for 'drop-in' learners.

Surveys had indicated a low level of training activity within local small businesses, and trainers working in South Shropshire suggested that local farmers were particularly unresponsive to invitations to join training programmes. However, with word-of-mouth publicity and announcements in church, the opening of the Vron IT centre in August 1996 was a spectacular success, with 400 people attending. After the opening, farmers' evenings and other similar events, with demonstrations of IT software and hardware, were well attended and training and other services taken up. Almost all courses have been fully subscribed at Newcastle. The high level of response from local people, women and farmers included, would seem to relate directly to the social role of the community centre as the focus of local networks. The community centre and its affiliated organisations are run by local people, many of whom are farmers or farmers' wives. The community centre being at the heart of the local community has meant the IT centre is on home territory and the local community feels a sense of ownership. The regular programme of events and activities has promoted a cross fertilisation resulting in greater use of the centre.

In its early years, the centre experienced difficulties because the promised funding for management staff did not materialise. The strains on the volunteer managers of the full-time programme were therefore considerable. Cash flow problems also put the centre in jeopardy. However, funding for management was obtained during the second year and there has been good progress towards the establishment of a viable teleworking operation, set up as a community-based charitable company. The centre staff are also supplying useful, low-cost consultancy services to local people, including small businesses. The development of teleworking, however, threatened to have an inhibiting effect upon the training function of the centre by limiting the centres use for training to evenings only. This problem has recently been alleviated by obtaining additional space for the training function.

Bishops Castle IT centre has been increasingly successful in the face of some initially negative dynamics in its planning and early development phase. Some aspects of the Rural Challenge Programme were controversial and this resulted in a change of management. It was felt that several local groups had a strong prior claim to the IT facility; these included the local secondary community school and a local trust with strong IT skills. Whilst being both popular and successful, the local community school was felt to be under threat of closure as a result of its relatively small size and the financial pressures on secondary education in Shropshire. The opening of the centre, managed by Rural Broadnet, was consequently low key, but early skills training sessions recruited well and the centre was well received by the local community.

The role of the centre was to offer access to IT equipment, education and training and support to businesses as well as the community. Its economic regeneration role was a major aspect of its work in a town that had lost jobs and industries over recent years. The centre formed part of the larger Enterprise House project which also offered small business units and office accommodation for new companies. The Bishop's Castle IT centre was a new institution, not part of local social networks, and it was therefore necessary to create an identity for it and to find ways of drawing in the wider community. As a new centre dealing in new technology, it needed to create new traditions and new patterns of usage. When the centre opened, community groups were invited to make visits. Those people with absolutely no computer experience were targeted for induction courses and training groups were easily filled. The centre ran an effective publicity campaign and set up family evenings to gain a wider exposure to the local community. Early training and family sessions were provided free of charge and recruited very well.

Since opening in December 1996, work with businesses has been targeted as a complimentary way of working with the local school which had an established programme of community education. A range of introductory courses for small business has been successful and a parallel business support scheme is in place. Of registered users, 25 per cent were self-employed, matching the proportion of sole traders registered in the area. Evidence indicated that the self-employed had higher levels of qualification than the average, and also that they worked longer hours and thus had less time available for training. It seemed clear that the local and flexible provision of courses was essential in order to enable this group to take up education or training opportunities. As the centre has become more established, it has increasingly fulfilled a much-needed, low-cost IT consultancy role for small businesses in the surrounding area, generating valuable income and helping the progression towards long-term financial viability.

Recently, following lengthy discussions with the county council, plans were agreed to move the local public library into a section of the Enterprise House building not previously refurbished since its use as a factory. The considerable synergy between the developing services of the library and the IT resource centre – in terms of books, texts, research information, public information systems, education and training – makes for a particularly exciting development. Footfall, particularly for the IT centre, should increase significantly.

Rural Broadnet has subsequently facilitated supported distance delivery of courses at these and other centres, using offline and online computer technology. These courses include the Cambridge Information Technology Certificate and a NVQ Level 2 in Childcare, both in collaboration with a FE provider and a voluntary sector project. There are also HE short courses, from the university's School of Computing and Information Technology (SCIT), dealing with the Internet, web page design and some programming languages. Educational guidance and information services have been delivered via Career Focus and project staff. The Wolverhampton University HE Shop delivers advice and guidance services into the area using video-conferencing. The intention is to integrate these and other guidance services more fully into the delivery programme. The development of Rural Broadnet's planned programme also involved facilitating supported distance learning through additional centres, including schools and an FE College. Currently there is a total of seven delivery venues.

The first HE short course selected by Rural Broadnet from the university's SCIT was the 'Welcome to the Internet' course, which had been originally prepared by the Broadnet project for use with Black Country companies. Broadnet was a broadband project, with high-capacity, dedicated ICT links which permitted fast access to the Internet and multimedia materials. Unfortunately it was not possible to access such material in rural areas where Internet connections were slow and equipment generally not of the highest specification. Rural Broadnet therefore decided to take a 'bottom-up' view of technical development and adapted freely-available, low-cost, tried-and-tested solutions that were viable for rural areas. Thus the online approach was rejected as being too expensive to run. The alternative was CD-based materials with paper back-up, on the assumption that rural ICT centres could afford to install a good 'entry level' computer with a CD drive. CD has the advantage of being able to hold large amounts of information and also allows the student to work directly on computer from the CD-based courseware. Online connections were utilised for submission and return of assignments. In collaboration with SCIT staff, the Internet course was rewritten for CD, piloted, revised and then launched as part of a very successful European Social Fund 5b programme.

The development of links with other IT centres led Rural Broadnet into working relationships with secondary schools in the north of the county and with the voluntary sector. Traditionally the voluntary sector is a 'Cinderella' sector, often poorly equipped and without access to appropriate training. Oswestry and District Helpmates (a volunteering organisation) had undertaken a training needs and skills analysis in its local area and, with Rural Broadnet's support, then embarked on developing a training programme. The idea of locally-delivered, ICT-supported, distance delivery appealed to Helpmates since many of its staff and volunteers had difficulty accessing traditional day-time provision and were likely to benefit from more flexible delivery. Courses in IT, Childcare (NVQ Level 2) and assessor training were arranged and facilitated in the Oswestry area, using a local secondary school as delivery venue. Local mentors were recruited and trained by Helpmates to provide support for the Childcare course. They proved effective in supporting students who were studying in a more individualised and dispersed way than with the IT courses. Rural Broadnet has also collaborated with Helpmates to establish an ICT training resource within the Helpmates project to improve flexibility of access to training facilities for students

Success and failure

As far as this project is concerned the key to success in attracting rural adult students back into education has been the local availability and flexible delivery of courses. Students have frequently emphasised the importance to them of the opportunity to study locally. Mothers with young children, carers and those running small businesses point out the difficulties they have in finding time to study. They have all welcomed the flexibility offered by a choice of evening or daytime study sessions at a local centre. They have also welcomed a regime that can accommodate gaps in study and allows for students to complete courses at their own pace.

Small businesses have used the training not only to develop IT skills but also to apply the skills in order to improve their business systems. The Internet and web-page design course has enabled some businesses to market their services to a much wider group of clients. In other cases, this course has proved a key in helping to identify new Internet-related business development opportunities as part of an economic diversification process. Rural Broadnet has established a collection of student web pages from the HE short course, over 70 of which are for small businesses. These include bed and breakfast, craft manufacture and sales, food based companies, a film services company and retail outlets such as bookshops. New Internet-based businesses include a roasted meat company specialising in spit-roasts, and diversification projects into Internet publishing of children's books, sales of tractors and home furnishings.

Collaboration with voluntary sector organisations has meant their networks of contacts have facilitated recruitment of students. These organisations have welcomed the flexibility of ICT-supported training and have pointed out, anecdotally, that some students who had negative schooling experience reported a preference for the relative 'privacy' of computer-based learning (CBL), where they felt they could risk 'failure' and not feel exposed before a group of peers.

The use of local mentors and support staff, particularly for the childcare course organised by Helpmates, proved highly successful in supporting students who were working in a non-synchronous group on an individual basis. In this case, the support extended by the mentors and NVQ assessors helped keep the group of students motivated and confident that they would succeed.

The most obvious failure in the project was, perhaps not surprisingly to those experienced in ICT, in relation to dealing with technical problems. In the early days, technical hitches with software and hardware caused some dislocation to the work of the centres. In the later stages, as networks, ISDN connections and Internet routing became more common, there were problems with these new elements of the technology. Technical support for Rural Broadnet was originally provided from the nearest university campus, 50 miles away. It became increasingly apparent that, with the best will in the world, busy technicians were unable to drop whatever they were doing in order to solve a problem in a rural centre over an hour away by car. Where an IT system was not functioning, a centre might grind to a complete halt to the frustration of its students. With IT there is no half measures: it either works or does not work. The solution to the problem was, by virtue of having attracted additional funding for our education and training work, to appoint a sufficiently skilled technician who would dedicate time to supporting Rural Broadnet's needs. This underlined the need for ICT-based projects to build the appropriate technical skills into their staffing. Such projects need to be realistically planned and costed and adequate technical support services have to be included in the budget.

Video-conferencing also proved more difficult to apply to Rural Broadnet's work than originally anticipated. The initial intention had been to experiment with the use of video-conferencing as a regular communications tool: to video-conference lectures to rural areas, to provide remote tutor support and to video-conference advice sessions. In the event, Rural Broadnet was successful in setting up HE advice and guidance sessions to a local school from the university's HE shop. University policy on purchasing decisions and technical problems, such as compatibility of different systems, also held back progress. It also became clear, from the experience of other universities, that the medium was proving less flexible than many had anticipated. In some cases, the video-conferencing systems had proved too cumbersome for students to use regularly. In other cases, where it had been used in an ambitious manner to link a tutor with a group of students or to link two groups of students, the medium proved too inflexible to maintain adequate communication.

The lesson from these experiences appeared to be that where the transaction is simple – for example, an advice session 'head-to-head' with two individuals sitting and static in front of a camera – then the medium had a good chance of success (as in advice and guidance). With groups, however, problems arose about who was in camera shot or who was in microphone range. It was clear that video-conferenced meetings needed to be very carefully structured if they were not to become confused, and worked best in expensive 'studio' settings. Being very structured might, of course, detract from the vitality of the meeting experience. It was also realised that the video-conferencing system would require exclusive access to a centre's ISDN line, and thus prohibit concurrent use of the line for other purposes, such as email and Internet access. Despite these reservations it is anticipated that, as the technology evolves, video-conferencing will become increasingly used in rural ICT learning systems (and particularly the Internet conferencing options, such as NetMeeting) and will facilitate provision of remote tutor support.

Methodologies for learning via ICT

The basic assumption of Rural Broadnet's work has been that to offer a wider range of FE and HE courses in rural areas, where students may study individually or in small and therefore 'uneconomic' groups, it is necessary to find a delivery methodology that does not rely on frequent face-to-face tutor contact. The supported distance delivery method therefore assumes that courseware materials will be locally delivered with local support staff or mentors, but without the face-to-face presence of a tutor at each session.

The provision of local face-to-face support is, of course, a key issue for students who return to learning. Rural Broadnet has provided such support via mentors, NVQ assessors and its own outreach workers. Local mentors may provide personal and pastoral support, and in some cases a degree of academic support. However, as far as ICT courses are concerned, Rural Broadnet's outreach workers, although not tutors, are knowledgeable in ICT and are therefore able to offer support to students in the local centres. As the curriculum expands and becomes increasingly wide and specialised, it is unlikely to be possible to find a range of suitable academic skills amongst local mentors within the community. Whilst developing the services of local mentor support, it will be necessary to facilitate remote access to active tutor support across a wider range of study areas, making online tutor links more interactive. It will also be necessary to offer student support through well-designed courseware and integrated support materials. These may include devices such as 'frequently asked questions' through links to supplementary study materials which offer additional explanation of particular topics or greater detail; and via multiple choice tests, which can help students assess the progress of their ongoing learning. However, synchronous virtual study groups will also require ready access to tutorial advice via an audio and visual link which includes the ability to share the computer desktop interactively, so that the students' work and tutor's explanation may be readily accessed by both parties.

As far as an increase in the range of curriculum material is concerned, it is important to recognise that not all subject areas are equally susceptible to CBL. Those unsuited to CBL delivery may include technical or scientific subjects that require practical laboratory or workshop sessions, or management subjects requiring applied learning in a practical management context. This is difficult to replicate through distance delivery because of the need for a degree of collaborative interaction. Other areas of 'people-skills' requiring group interaction to facilitate learning are also likely to prove less susceptible to delivery via ICT. In the case of field courses, the multimedia resources of IT have been deployed with some success to simulate practical experience. However there is continuing debate on how far simulations can replace exposure to the actual experience of the field course.

Student-centred learning via ICT

Many educators in CE assume that an emphasis on ICT-supported learning is necessarily in conflict with a learner-centred approach. However there is a strong case for suggesting that ICT as a learning vehicle increases the range and quality of learning resources available to individuals and offers an enhanced learner-centred approach. Salmon discusses the learner-centred approach influenced by Carl Rogers and adopted by the Open University Business School, which 'has been concerned from the beginning to adopt broadly constructivist methods in tutoring and to avoid transmission views of management teaching. It puts the student firmly in the frame as an active meaningmaker who comes to the learning on the course with an existing store of knowledge.'[4] The information resources of the Internet, the design capabilities of computer-aided design systems, music-making programmes and numerous other facilities offer individual students the possibility of self-directed, individualised learning programmes which allow them to research topics or explore their chosen fields of learning to advanced levels. As Sulla argues in relation to ICT-based learning in secondary education:

> If we consider the wider picture of education, computer technology provides students and teachers with unprecedented opportunities to transform the teaching and learning process, from the most common and simple uses to the most sophisticated. Word processing eliminates endless hand copying and allows teachers and students to place a greater emphasis on content revision. Graphing software eliminates hand-drawing of equation results and allows teachers and students to focus on the effects of various changes in an equation. The Internet greatly reduces the time and effort it used to take to locate information on a topic, and puts students and teachers in touch with other students and teachers around the world, as well as with content experts … With all this vast potential at their fingertips, the challenge to educators today is not to use computers, but to infuse computer use into the instructional setting. A two-part approach of problem-based learning and facilitation does much to promote technology infusion.[5]

If CE does not embrace the opportunities offered by ICT-based learning, then it risks losing touch with mainstream development and depriving its student cohorts of wider learning opportunities. Smart *et al.* describes the changes in mainstream HE:

> Students are becoming much more demanding and responsive in terms of technology use. Best practice recognises that conventional lectures are relatively ineffective in terms of providing an opportunity for learning … Accordingly lecturers are increasingly deploying student-centred activities in lectures that encourage the students to reflect on the lecture content. Computers can and should be used to provide multimedia illustrations of concepts … including images, diagrams, animations, video and sound. While all these media can be delivered individually without a computer, current presentation software also allows them to be integrated into a single presentation.[6]

An ICT-based approach requires investment in new learning resources and a change in methodology for the tutor. In practice one of the greatest obstacles to the introduction of ICT-supported learning is the resistance of teaching staff. Littlejohn and Stefani have described one of the barriers as the skills gap:

> One of these perceived barriers can be articulated simply as the 'skills gap', which exists for both staff and students with respect to effective use of C&IT. At a deeper level this particular barrier can be expressed in terms of many academic staff showing a lack of understanding of their pedagogical role in a C&IT-based instructional environment. This interpretation is based on comments from many staff who display a reluctance to adopt teaching strategies that are different from those which they themselves experienced, and a difficulty in acknowledging a theoretical underpinning of teaching and learning strategies.[7]

For the successful delivery of ICT-based learning, staff will need professional development in the use of the technology and the provision of online support to students. Salmon has analysed the role of the 'moderator' in relation to online learning and has highlighted the key principles.[8] These include 'housekeeping' aspects relating to the practice of online support and facilitation. Examples include continuity issues, such as visiting the web-based materials often; ensuring continuity of virtual conferences; the need for good layout and easy navigation of virtual materials; and the need to facilitate emergence of new topics and deletion of redundant materials to maintain momentum but avoid overload. These are all skills that have parallels in traditional methodology Salmon emphasises the need for thorough training in all aspects of online work for staff and students before such development is undertaken.

Government policy on ICT and learning

The movement of government policy in the direction of embracing ICT to enhance learning at all levels within the mainstream education system has spawned a number of initiatives. The National Grid for Learning (NGfL), University for Industry (UfI) and the e-University lead clearly in this direction. Learning Partnerships are being encouraged to recognise the potential of CBL. Initiatives such as the Higher Education Reach Out to Business and the Community Fund (HEROBaC) are also broadening the focus of university work and have much to gain from ICT-based solutions; for example, in work-based learning and communications links. The Capital Modernisation Fund and Adult and Community Learning Fund are providing support for the development of local ICT centres as community learning resources. This level of government support for ICT initiatives is to be welcomed and offers support to the HE sector and also to community-based ICT centres.

Governments are attracted by the 'big idea' which they believe may have a transforming effect upon education – and certainly NGfL and UfI have the potential to effect such transformations. However, there are dangers in such 'top down', broad-brush approaches where ICT is concerned. ICT implementation is a detailed and precise process, and planning for implementation requires an absolute knowledge of what the technology can do if there is to be ultimate success. In practice, both NGfL and UfI have experienced difficulties with implementation. With NGfL, the rate of progress within individual schools appears to be conditioned either by the quality and level of support from the local authority or, if local authority support is poor, by the level of ICT skills available within the particular school. Where neither is available, schools have struggled to deal with the complexities of network technology and to devise systems for using the potential of ICT-based learning. In the case of UfI, basic misunderstandings about the lack of suitability of the Internet as a medium for transmitting a mass learning system have surfaced from within. Widespread concern has been voiced about other aspects of the scheme from participating agencies during the preparation phase of the project. With both schemes, there appears to have been a lack of sufficient prior consideration of the educational and technical methodology required to make the systems work satisfactorily. In the longer term, however, both NGfL and UfI are likely to become increasingly influential in the delivery of mainstream education, offering new opportunities and enhancing the scale and scope of the learning experience. As such, these developments should be applauded and their significance for rural areas carefully evaluated.

Conclusions: sustainability, diversification, community development and andragogy

Over the life of the Rural Broadnet project, diversification has been increasingly identified as a key response to the issue of sustainability, both for rural ICT centres as well as for the rural economy generally – particularly farm related businesses. For the latter, the recent crises in the agricultural economy have brought an increasing number of businesses (particularly in marginal farming areas such as the Marches) to the point where they are no longer viable. In order to sustain these businesses, owners have looked to develop second or third income streams by diversifying into new commercial developments. During this period the role of economic regeneration in rural areas has included helping to sustain existing companies by enabling their owners to diversify into other concurrent activities.

Similarly, diversification has become an important principle for the rural ICT centres. As a response to local needs, Rural Broadnet initially opted to develop and work with community-based centres, rather than with traditional adult and community education centres. In practice, they have offered more flexible learning opportunities than local schools, especially where daytime access is essential. However, lacking the wider resources of schools or colleges, they have needed to develop solid income streams to become sustainable. Through diversification, they have extended the range of their activities and have added corporate training and advice and consultancy on a full range of ICT topics to their normal training programmes. This broader range of activities has enabled both centres to move positively towards financial sustainability.

Through economic regeneration work, the original community development emphasis of the project has become a major element in Rural Broadnet's activities. Community development in the developed world has focussed primarily on issues of urban deprivation – where programmes have addressed improvements in quality of life, social and support facilities, with some emphasis on training and (more rarely) on community industry and creation of jobs. The colonial origins of community development in the 1940s was based on work programmes dealing with economic development, education and primary healthcare issues and was often located in rural areas where communities were stable but impoverished. Rural Broadnet's activity has been closer to this original model in providing support to rural communities through economic regeneration. The project has responded to the 'felt needs' of local communities through partnerships with local schools, colleges and funding agencies to provide relevant IT skills for rural areas.

It can be argued that the facilities and training programmes of the new ICT centres have contributed to the empowerment of local people and local communities. Access to IT and Internet skills impacts on a number of levels: it can provide new and wider training opportunities; improve career prospects; enhance SME performance; and stimulate new business development, including community enterprise. It can help to address the deficit of the IT 'have nots', the rural disadvantaged and the older generation who were not schooled in IT. More generally, it can help to overcome some of the disadvantages of rural isolation by providing a cheap and fast communications medium for sending and receiving an immense range of information, documents, designs and data. The acquisition of key skills in IT offers empowering opportunities in terms of information and knowledge for people in rural areas.

The development of ICT-based learning is likely, in the longer term, to be of major significance for adult learners, perhaps comparable with the introduction of the Open University. The spread of ICT learning networks, plus the increased availability of a broad range of curriculum materials capable of remote delivery, has all the potential for effecting major changes in rural education and training. Rural learners, whether undertaking 'returner' courses, mainstream degree courses or shorter continuing professional development programmes, will have an increasing choice of learning options.

ICT has the potential to impact in a major way on the wider needs of rural areas by providing a vital and influential communications medium, with empowering facilities that can reach into the economic and social lives of rural dwellers. Already it has facilitated the development of ICT-based rural enterprises that offer new opportunities to sustain the rural economy. It can also play an important part in revitalising rural facilities and service provision to increase the empowerment of rural communities, allowing them more control over their lives and a greater level of self-determination in decision making. Whilst the needs of the IT 'have-nots' are yet to be fully addressed, rural widening participation funding offers the possibility of doing so.

Without these ICT developments the prospects for rural areas would be poor indeed. The questions for rural continuing educators are how far they recognise the significance of ICT-based learning – and how far they are prepared, or able, to utilise the technology to benefit their learners. This is not simply a question of delivering courses via ICT. It is also a matter of ensuring that appropriate IT skills are in place for staff and students; of providing networks of support (including local mentors and ICT remote tutor support) for a wider curriculum; and of facilitating access to the hardware and software which can enable learners to be self-directed in research, learning and communication. With appropriate advice and guidance, ICT-based education and information systems offer continuing educators the prospect of a radically enhanced provision for rural learners in the twenty-first century.

Notes

1. University of Wolverhampton Business School (1995). *Bishop's Castle and District Rural Challenge Business Survey*. University of Wolverhampton.
2. Shropshire Chamber of Commerce, Training & Enterprise (1997). *Household Survey*.
3. Knowles, M. (1990). *The Adult Learner*. Gulf Publishing.
4. Salmon, G. (1998). Developing learning through effective online moderation. *Active Learning*, no. 9. December: pp. 3–8.
5. Sulla, N. *Technology: To Use or Infuse*. Technology Source. http://horizon.unc.edu/TS/commentary/1999-02.asp. Accessed 6 January 2001.
6. Smart, C., Miller, P., Essaka, M., Young, C. and Wonnacott, D. (2000). *Producing Computer-Based Presentations for the Lecture Theatre or the Web*. CTI Centre for History, Archaeology & Art History, University of Glasgow.
7. Littlejohn, A.H. and Stefani, L.J. (1999). Effective use of communication and information technology: bridging the skills gap. *Association for Learning Technology Journal*; vol. 7.2: pp. 66–76.
8. Salmon, *op. cit.*

9

A third-age rural learners' project

Marie Askam

Introduction

If we genuinely subscribe to the ideal of lifelong learning and to humanistic concepts of equality of opportunity, we need to address ourselves to considering the relationship between continuing education and the quality of life – however this is defined – of older people who can no longer be neatly classified as those past statutory retirement age.[1]

A dominant view among social policy makers and educationalists is that lifelong learning is beneficial to the individuals who engage in it and to society at large. Learning should not finish when an individual leaves formal education but should continue throughout life. It is perhaps particularly important that older people should have access to continuing education (CE). Not least are the issues of equality of opportunity and social inclusion; education should not be perceived solely as the prerogative of the young or those in paid employment.

The implications of a rapidly ageing population are manifold. In practical terms, more older people might be encouraged in the future to continue in full- or part-time paid employment because there will be insufficient younger workers to maintain them. Education will be necessary to up-date older people's skills and knowledge and there is evidence to suggest that many would welcome this opportunity to extend their working lives. CE can contribute greatly to the quality of life of many older people who may retire earlier and live longer than previous generations. Older people who are actively engaged in learning programmes are less likely to suffer from illness and depression and make fewer demands on social and health services.

This chapter discusses a third-age rural learners' project organised by the University of Cambridge Board of Continuing Education. We had seen what had been achieved by other institutions, such as the Senior Studies Institute at the University of Strathclyde in Glasgow and the Retirement Centre in Bedford, and we wished to make our own contribution to the field. The project was therefore designed specifically to signal a commitment to lifelong learning by offering equality of opportunity to third-age learners. The aims of the project were to reach out to older learners and encourage them to participate in university CE through the provision of a stimulating and appropriate programme of courses; to contribute to the quality of life of older people; to learn more about identifying and meeting the needs of older learners; and to encourage older learners to make a long-term commitment to CE. Withnall refers to the need 'to address ourselves to considering the relationship between continuing education and the quality of life'. Awareness of this relationship underpinned the project from beginning to end.[2]

Rurality was a secondary issue that reflected the Board's geographical location: in an extensive and essentially rural area with relatively isolated areas of existing provision for university CE. Public transport in this area is generally so poor that individuals without cars have difficulty in getting to urban centres. This applies particularly to older learners who may be unable to drive, do not have access to a car or are unwilling to drive into urban areas, especially at night.

The project, funded by the Higher Education Funding Council for England (HEFCE), ran from 1995–99 and took the form of a comparative study between two rural areas within the Board of Continuing Education's region. Within each area we planned a liberal arts programme of short, non-accredited courses in six newly-established centres. Costs were to be kept as low as possible in order to facilitate participation. The first year of the comparative study was to be 1997. The period from January to August was to be spent in preparation: choosing the precise locations within the broadly-prescribed areas; selecting six appropriate centres; devising a study-programme of six liberal arts courses to run at the six centres; engaging tutors and organising publicity to attract local interest and support. The courses were to run during the autumn term, and the following year (1998) the whole process would be repeated in the second area chosen for the study. The project ended in July 1999.

This chapter describes the development and evolution of the project and evaluates its successes and failures. It looks beyond the project and considers the prospects for embedding the activity. It details some unexpected outcomes of the work and it looks back over the past four years to draw a number of broad conclusions. The emphasis is on the practical application of the aims agreed with the funding council. The project was composed of two central elements: the rural locations in which the comparative study was conducted and the older learners – who were the target-group – defined by the project as post-50 or third-age students. A rural area was defined as one in which students' access to the educational opportunities offered by the urban centres was limited and where there was little existing provision of CE. These twin strands, the rural and the third age, are the central theme of the chapter.

The rural dimension

As the project's rural outreach worker, my initial tasks included selecting a specific project area in both Bedfordshire and Hertfordshire and choosing six suitable centres within each of these two areas. Parish magazines were an important part of this selection process. They convey a great deal about a village's atmosphere and can help in assessing potential levels of receptiveness to new activities such as those that our project would offer. Not all villages produce a regular magazine or newsletter – a possible indication of low levels of community activity. From a practical perspective, this meant that a vital method of disseminating information about the project locally would be unavailable. In the final choice of villages we favoured those with parish magazines or newsletters produced on a frequent and regular basis, well distributed in the community and widely available in local shops and other appropriate centres. This meant that small, remote communities were rejected in favour of larger, more vibrant villages. We were aware that this seemed incongruous in a project dedicated to outreach work. However we needed to ensure as far as possible that the courses would not founder through lack of support. We also hoped that individuals in the more remote communities would be able to organise transport to these larger centres.

The areas chosen were fairly small, comprising six connected small towns or large villages, so that the programme could be presented as an integrated whole rather than a discrete and seemingly random scattering of courses over a wider area. An integrated programme would have more impact, publicity would be easier and more effective and local residents might be persuaded to attend more than one course if distances between centres were short. It would enable me to visit several centres during the course of one session. This strategy also meant that I could function more efficiently. The first comparative study area chosen was to the south east of Bedford, an area characterised by small market towns and villages, with no large towns or motorways and seemingly plenty of opportunity for increased CE provision.

The rural dimension influenced many elements of the project. The most quantifiable influences included choice of centres, programmes of study, availability of resources and tutors and transport to centres. It is likely that there were other less apparent influences such as family connections and strong social networks within certain village communities. However these might also have existed within the framework of an urban comparative study.

Choice of centres was directly affected by rural setting. There were few schools and no large educational establishments. However I had already decided against using such official territory believing that the project would have a better chance of success if venues which belonged to the wider community were used – such as parish rooms, church halls, libraries and small museums. We hoped this policy would encourage both older learners with experience of CE, and those without, for whom school buildings might hold negative associations. The twelve new centres included five village halls, two parish rooms, two libraries, one church room, one community centre and one museum.

One outcome of this policy was that hiring charges were low: an important factor, since our venture was non-profit making and costs had to be passed on to students. This helped us to keep our fees low. Apart from the libraries, most of these venues lacked the sophisticated facilities to which many tutors have grown accustomed, offering only tables and chairs. All portable equipment needed to be ordered in advance from the Board and collected and returned by the tutors or myself. Book-boxes, containing relevant books for each course from the Board's library, needed to be posted at considerable expense, or again delivered and returned by the same means. Moreover, all the centres were in constant use, which meant that the Board's equipment needed to be taken home after every session by the tutors. Most of the centres were organised so that each activity was allotted a particular slot during the week and would not be disturbed. Only in one centre did several activities run simultaneously, so that the tutor had to hold the students attention against a background of piano accompaniment to a children's dancing class in the room below. Seen from the students' point of view, however, such proximity to other learners gave the positive message that here was lifelong learning happening in the community.

It became clear that the tutors chosen for the programme should be creative, resourceful and adaptable. Their role (discussed further below) was crucial in determining the success of the project. All the tutors were happy with the limitations imposed by the rural centres and all met the challenges. Another critical issue that became increasingly apparent, as affecting both tutors and students, was that of transport in rural areas. Whalley refers to this problem in her report on rural third-age learners in the Cotswolds.[3] Unless our tutors lived in the villages or small towns where their courses were to run, access to a car would be essential since public transport was inadequate.

Identifying and meeting the needs of older learners

Adult educators must make a rigorous examination of their theory and practice in relation to older adults, and seek, with them, both the breaking down of stereotypes of ageing and the self-empowerment of older people themselves. Ways must continue to be found to liberate the elders (to coin a phrase of the 1970s) and to enable the elders to liberate themselves.[4]

Many practitioners working with older learners stress that they do not comprise a homogeneous group. However Bornat identifies a significant paradox.[5] She argues that 'older people are an aggregate of infinitely diverse individuals', but they are also 'a group or a class.' She continues: 'These two propositions are not mutually exclusive because they enable us to reflect on issues (e.g. older people as learners) from different hypothetical standpoints rather than forming two explanations of the position of older people in the real world.' Our target group was to be older learners and they would come from different socio-economic backgrounds, with differing experiences and expectations of lifelong learning, but age itself would unite them, according to Bornat. They would also have a unifying rural background.

In terms of age, the majority of participants in the study were 50 years or older. Of equal significance is that the oldest participating student was 90 years old, 40 years older than the youngest participant. This age difference, at any stage in adult life, has profound implications. Therefore, while it was helpful to think of the target group both as heterogeneous and homogeneous, it was important to recognise the limitations of any kind of labelling. Withnall and Percy argue: 'It is important to avoid making assumptions about the potential and motivation of older people to become learners at any age and thus to avoid labelling provision in certain restrictive ways.'[6]

Nevertheless, the academic community commonly refers to older learners as a group. The project named them as its target group, and I needed to work with this concept whilst also bearing in mind its limitations. It was helpful to return to Bornat's paradox from time to time since, despite its limitations, the concept of older learners had some meaning. A major challenge for the project was to provide courses that would be intellectually challenging but not intimidating. Emphasising the heterogencity of third-age learners, Schuller and Walker argue that: 'Educational provision should be as wide-ranging as possible.'[7] Groombridge echoes this and adds: 'The programme devised should provide an open-ended opportunity for study, enabling students to feel supported and to develop greater self confidence and assurance as learners.'[8] Shea stresses the need to acknowledge and use the experience of older learners: 'It would be a waste not to try to utilise their vast experience of life as a resource for the class, and not to use the skills they already have.'[9] The curriculum therefore needed to acknowledge older learners as a heterogeneous group and reflect this in a varied programme. It needed to recognise and draw on older learners' existing skills and experience and generate increasing confidence and self-empowerment in the target-group. Since the courses were non-accredited, they could be open-ended, having no assessment criteria to meet. Within the liberal arts framework stipulated by the project, two study programmes were devised, each with six courses.

Width and variety of provision were central aims, although the rural setting also exerted its own influence. Courses needed to relate to the putative students' frame of reference in the rural community and were devised to draw heavily on local landscape and history. We particularly wanted to avoid what might be perceived as lofty and irrelevant topics. Course titles needed to be inviting and relevant to older learners in the local community; they needed to be challenging but avoid potentially intimidating academic terminology. It was also important to consider the areas of expertise offered by tutors. Courses evolved which reflected the three following criteria: subject areas which would be of interest to older learners; those which drew on local landscape and history; and tutors' expertise. Since we attempted to use older tutors to underpin our commitment to lifelong learning, especially those that lived in the areas chosen for the comparative study, it was not difficult to meet these criteria. The courses offered in Bedfordshire were:

1. Discovering Bedfordshire's Old Buildings
2. Parks and Woodlands of the Greensand Ridge
3. The Cottage Industries of Bedfordshire
4. Bedfordshire in the 1940s
5. Creative Writing Through Living Memory
6. Towns and Villages of Mid-Bedfordshire.

Hertfordshire courses were devised to meet the same three criteria. They were:

1. Markets, Auctions and Fairs in Royston
2. Gardens and Mazes of East Anglia
3. Hertfordshire Countryside Customs of the 19th Century
4. Braughing Oral History
5. Villages of East Hertfordshire
6. Researching Your Family History.

Each class was specifically selected for an individual centre in order to exploit existing historical and geographical features of the immediate locality and to reflect its activities and interests. Selecting tutors whose approach to teaching would meet the needs of older learners was of vital importance since, however inviting the study programme, it would only succeed if appropriately taught. The Carnegie Inquiry into the Third Age refers to evidence which suggests that 'older people can learn as well as younger ones provided learning is self-pacing and practical rather than by memorising instructions, and builds on previous experience.'[10] This recognition was central to the teaching of the programme. Schuller and Walker make a plea for 'imaginative training for those working in the field',[11] but it was not possible for us to undertake such training in the context of the project, although this could be incorporated into a broader programme of staff development offered by the Board at a later date. We needed to work with tutors with no particular training in the teaching of third-age learners.

From our perspective, a more helpful point made by Schuller and Walker was that: 'The potential of older people as learners and as teachers should be fully recognised.'[12] Recognising that older teachers can provide good role models for older students and might be better equipped to identify and meet their needs guided us towards employing as many older tutors as possible. We also looked for non-didactic tutors who would work towards increasing student confidence through a carefully structured programme – allowing students to proceed at their own pace and encouraging them to contribute their own knowledge and experience. Tutors therefore needed to view their students as a resource, project a positive attitude towards older people as teachers and learners (and to ageing itself), and work towards self-empowerment and autonomy for their students.

Most of the students preferred daytime classes[13] and we therefore ran all our classes between 2.00 and 4.00 p.m. and ensured that tutors allowed time for a tea break during the session. Since over one-third of people aged 55 and over in England live alone,[14] the tea break served a dual purpose. It provided an opportunity for social engagement and fostered group cohesion, thus contributing to the overall success of the programme. We ended both programmes in Bedfordshire and Hertfordshire with tea and mince pies and all participants – tutors, students and any members of the community who had been particularly helpful – were invited. These primarily social occasions also allowed us to thank all those who had contributed to the programmes' success and gave an informal opportunity for feedback from the students which could be added to the more measured feedback provided by the students on evaluation forms.

Assessing and embedding the project

A wide range of barriers exist which depress people's aspirations and participation: attitudes of the clientele, employers, providers and society at large; timing, location and physical environment of classes; lack of information and guidance; money.[15]

When both study programmes had been delivered, we were able to make comparisons between them and assess the extent to which we had succeeded in our initial aim. Success was to be defined in terms of the numbers of rural third-age students who attended these classes. We also needed to consider the embedding of the activity, which the funding body was especially keen to see implemented. In Bedfordshire during the autumn of 1997 four of the six planned ten-week courses ran with an average of eight students. In Hertfordshire the following autumn five classes ran with an average of 16.4 students. All courses in both counties had excellent attendance.

In all, 114 students took the courses we offered, 98 per cent of whom came from the surrounding rural environment of small market towns and villages. Seventy-six per cent of these students declared themselves to be post-50, although we believe that a much higher percentage complied with this criterion. Those who registered for the courses attended well throughout. These figures suggest that the project succeeded in its primary aim of encouraging third-age learners in rural areas to participate in university CE.

Yet subsequent reflection poses certain doubts and questions about the long-term benefits of such a project to the rural community. There is a marked discrepancy between the numbers of participants in the comparative study: twice the number of students took courses in Hertfordshire than in Bedfordshire, although parity in every respect, as far as possible, had been the aim. Apart from geographical location and possible socio-economic differences of which we are unaware, the only significance seems to be the timing of the study. The Bedfordshire programme ran during the autumn of 1997, and throughout the year – from January to December – contacts were made and valuable experience gained which could be deployed the following year in Hertfordshire, thus making genuine parity impossible to achieve. The project did not allow us the time to investigate this disparity in participation, so that we can only guess at possible reasons. Furthermore, a project that does not facilitate the opportunity to consolidate and build on activity in the rural community has an arbitrary quality. This is at odds with the open-ended, long-term work that needs to underpin the kind of embedding envisaged.

The Carnegie Inquiry draws attention to another barrier to embedding: 'Extra-mural departments may not maintain special outreach work with the possible end of earmarked funding.'[16] Throughout the four years of the project, many valuable contacts have been made. University CE has been taken into rural areas and local older learners' interest aroused and confidence gained. But previous levels of activity cannot be maintained when funding comes to an end. Students' progression is therefore exceedingly difficult to monitor and there will not be the funding for the post-course guidance and counselling advocated by Schuller and Walker as corollaries to good provision.[17] Other providers might do this, but the advantages for the students of continuity and familiarity with the initial provider will be lost; implications of this disruption at a crucial stage of progression are that students may be less likely to move on in CE.

The project must also be seen in a context of social inclusion when appraising its short- and long-term success. Whether or not embedding of the activity takes place, it is important to consider the immediate impact of the programme in the rural community on third-age learners. The 1999 United Nations International Year of Older Persons included the objective to: 'Engage the academic community in the exploration of the principles and practices of an age-integrated society.'[18] In its 'Principles for Older Persons,' older learners' needs are listed under 'Independence... Older persons should have access to appropriate educational and training programmes' and 'Self-fulfilment... Older persons should have access to the educational, cultural, spiritual and recreational resources of society.'[19]

However the social reality is that lack of money prevents participation in lifelong learning for many older people. The Joseph Rowntree Foundation reveals that: 'Thirty per cent of pensioners are in the bottom fifth of the income distribution and 1.5 million live off state pensions and benefits alone.'[20] It goes on to state that: 'Although old age is no longer synonymous with poverty, 60 per cent of pensioners are in the bottom 40 per cent of the income distribution.' The consequence is that 'pensioners are disproportionately represented among the poorest.' To counter such inequity, Carlton and Soulsby argue for 'equitable funding mechanisms to support learners according to their needs, in both part-time and full-time programmes, through Individual Learning Accounts, with disadvantaged older adults as a priority target.'[21] Schuller and Walker add that: 'Material support should be given to students on the one hand and to providers on the other, to encourage demand and to stimulate supply.'[22]

The fees for our courses were kept as low as possible, although we do not know how many additional older learners would have participated if financial assistance had been available. There are also the four million pensioners suffering from long-term illness or disability, and the five million who feel unsafe out alone after dark.[23] Older learners from these groups may have found that additional support was necessary to enable them to participate but the funding for our project did not allow for this.

A substantial difficulty was that of transport. While the lack of suitable public transport was less of a problem for those tutors who had paid work and access to a car, it was more of a potential problem for the categories of older people referred to in the Rowntree Findings living on low incomes or state pensions and denied car ownership. The rural location, a key feature of our project, heavily favoured car owners. Older learners not living within easy walking distance of centres and without access to cars, or the possibility of lifts to and from classes, would have found this difficulty a huge barrier. Again, when assessing the success of our project, we did not know the extent to which additional funding for transport would have enabled more people to participate.

One of the unexpected outcomes was that another local provider made contact with us. This led to a joint venture for Adult Learners' Week when we collaborated to run a day of courses designed for older learners. Three tutors who had taught on the Bedfordshire and Hertfordshire programmes gave 'taster' courses, free of charge, which were well received – each course running with an average of nine students. A Sunday morning walk around Cambridge earlier in the summer with 40 third-age learners from Prague, en route from Stevenage to Glasgow, came about when a Bedfordshire colleague contacted me to ask if I could arrange a walk for this group of people whose leader she had met on a recent visit to Prague. The result was an exceptionally enjoyable morning and an unexpected opportunity to discuss the work that is underway in both our countries with older learners. A future development may be an exchange between the Board's older learners in Cambridge and older learners in Prague.

Another unexpected and memorable learning experience came from a class that comprised older learners but included a younger woman with a baby. I was apprehensive that the baby might disturb the older students. However my fears were groundless: the younger student and the older students supported each other and the baby became a much-valued member of the group. It might be argued that such intergenerational co-operation undermines the value of courses designed for older learners, but it need not do so. The older students dominated the group in terms of numbers, and their needs within it were paramount; they were able to absorb one young mother and child without jeopardising their own educational needs. It would be more difficult to meet older learners' needs in an age-inclusive context.

Conclusions

During the course of the project I have learnt most from the older learners themselves; individuals primarily, but also as a group. Bornat's seemingly paradoxical view of older people as 'an aggregate of infinitely diverse individuals' as well as 'a group or class' was upheld. The students differed from each other in many ways that included marital status; family circumstances; material wealth; educational and professional background; and personality and personal preferences. Difference in age created its own diversity, although it was not the case that the age range was too broad since this was just one of many differences. Furthermore, individual energy and agility, physical and mental, differed greatly and was not directly correlated to chronological age. The students were as diverse as one would expect any group enrolling for the same course to be. Nonetheless, one factor united them: they were no longer young. All had reached or were approaching the end of paid employment; none had young families; all had passed the expected mid-point of life; many were grandparents. It was this that transformed them into a group.

As the project came to an end, I felt profound regret that the work could not continue. However, one of the Hertfordshire courses was so well received by its community that it will continue as an autonomous group. The work produced by the Oral History course in Braughing was so prolific and of such high quality that a book is now in production. Those who registered on the course and produced the material for the book will continue independently as the Braughing Oral History Group. A further lasting reminder of the inestimable value of lifelong learning, if one were needed, is the article contributed by the 90-year-old student, on the beneficial impact of adult CE on her own life, to the Board's *Ad Lib: Journal for Continuing Liberal Adult Education*.[24] This, and other more anecdotal evidence, strongly suggests that the project helped to foster confidence and self-empowerment among participants. Many reported an increase in confidence and many more demonstrated increasing autonomy by taking responsibility for their own learning in areas such as those cited above.

Despite misgivings regarding barriers to participation, created by factors that include low income and lack of public transport, I believe that ultimately the project has been worthwhile for all of us who participated. It represents progress, but much, much more work needs to be done. The Carnegie Enquiry argues: 'Education needs to be thought of as a lifelong activity, and there needs to be a strategic shift from full-time, initial education for the most advantaged towards part-time, lifelong, relatively cheap and accessible provision for all.'[25] The project endorses this view.

Notes

1. Withnall, A. (1990). In Glendenning, F. and Percy, K. eds. *Ageing, Education and Society: Readings in Educational Gerontology*. Association for Educational Gerontology; p. 47.
2. Withnall, *op. cit.*

3. Whalley, M. (1995). *The Education and Training Needs of Older Learners in the North Cotswolds (Gloucestershire) Full Report*. Gloucestershire College of Arts and Technology; p. 16.
4. Glendenning, F. (1990). In Glendenning and Percy, *op. cit.*, p. 20.
5. Bornat, J. (1990). In Glendenning and Percy, *op. cit.*, p. 96.
6. Withnall, A. and Percy, K. (1994). *Good Practice in the Education and Training of Older Adults*. Arena; p. 167.
7. Schuller, T. and Walker, A. (1990). *The time, of our life: education, employment and retirement in the third age*. Institute for Public Policy Research Employment Paper. no. 2; p. 22.
8. Groombridge, B. (1990). In Glendenning and Percy, *op. cit.*, pp. 180–1.
9. Shea, P. (1990). In Glendenning and Percy, *op. cit.*, p. 79.
10. The Carnegie United Kingdom Trust (1993). *The Carnegie Inquiry into the Third Age: Life, Work and Livelihood in the Third Age*; p. 53.
11. Schuller and Walker, *op. cit.*, p. 22.
12. *Ibid.*
13. Groombridge, *op. cit.*, p. 181.
14. Carlton, S. and Soulsby, J. (1999). *Learning to Grow Older and Bolder: A policy discussion paper on learning in later life*. NIACE; p. 16.
15. Carnegie Inquiry, *op. cit.*, p. 53.
16. *Ibid.*
17. Schuller and Walker, *op. cit.*, p. 53.
18. United Nations Department of Public Information (1998). *Towards a Society for All Ages: International Year of Older Persons 1999*. New York; April, p.1.
19. United Nations European Resource Unit (1998). *The United Nations and Older People*; pp. 2–3.
20. Joseph Rowntree Foundation (1998). Monitoring poverty and social exclusion. *Findings*. December; pp. 1–6.
21. Carlton and Soulsby, *op, cit.*, p. 81.
22. Schuller and Walker, *op, cit.*, p. 22.
23. Joseph Rowntree Foundation, *op. cit.*, p. 6.
24. *Ad Lib: Journal for Continuing Liberal Adult Education* (1999). University of Cambridge Board of Continuing Education; February, p. 7.
25. Carnegie Inquiry, *op. cit.*, p.57.

10

The Fenland Oral History Project

Susan Oosthuizen

Introduction

The Fenland Oral History Project (FOHP) focussed on encouraging older students living in the Cambridgeshire Fens (where there was no locally-delivered higher education [HE]) to enter into and progress within adult HE and continuing education (CE). The emphasis of the project was on local people, especially those who had not participated in HE before (and particularly women) and on developing strategies using non-accredited courses. For reasons of andragogy and inclusiveness the project used oral history, from the bidding process through to delivery, as its central strategy. The project was funded by a successful bid made in 1995 by the University of Cambridge Board of Continuing Education for widened participation funding from the Higher Education Funding Council for England (HEFCE).

The project's central problem was its need to address a major local barrier to participation in HE: a defensive regional culture, the result of a long history of a mistaken perception of Fenland 'backwardness'. This chapter begins by describing the wider background to the project and more generic barriers to learning presented by Fenland rurality. These especially relate to problems of age, poverty and lack of transport. The chapter then examines the generic and locally-specific cultural barriers to development work in the region before moving to the strategies employed to address these barriers. It concludes with an evaluation of the project's success.

The Fenland context

The Cambridgeshire Fens are bounded to the south by the River Ouse and to the north by the Wash (see Figure 1). The River Lark forms much of their eastern boundary, while the western edge lies along a line marked roughly by Peterborough and Crowland. The Fens extend into Lincolnshire, Northamptonshire, Suffolk and Norfolk, but these areas were excluded from the project since they fell within areas served by other providers.

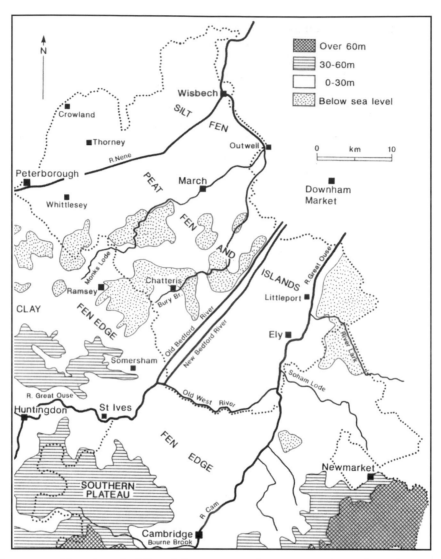

Figure 1. The Cambridgeshire Fens: places mentioned in the text

In this rural region, settlement and economy are heavily influenced by topography. Considerable areas lie at, or below, flood level and are not generally available for settlement. Population therefore tends to be concentrated in centres on the Fen edges (Ramsey, Peterborough, Downham Market), on islands standing above flood level in south and central Fenland (Ely, Chatteris, March, Whittlesey) and on a broad band of higher siltland lying between Spalding, Wisbech and King's Lynn. Outside these areas there is some settlement in isolated farmhouses and cottages.

The region's economy is predominantly agricultural. Poor road communications across the Fenland have retarded the development of new industry and commerce. This was exacerbated both by the closure of the railway centre in March, once the largest in Europe, and the recessions of the last 25 years. Industrial activity occurs where there is good access to communications and this tends today to be along the borders – for example, in Peterborough, a rapidly expanding urban area with its own Development Corporation. There is some industrial activity in Wisbech, where the port and Elgood's Brewery are among the major employers.

The 1991 Census showed that the Fenland has the largest proportion (21.4 per cent) of people of pensionable age in Cambridgeshire, a proportion that increased since 1981, following national trends.[1] A relatively high (28 per cent) and growing proportion of households contain only pensioners, with many consisting of one pensioner living alone.[2] Another 17.1 per cent are aged between 45 and 59 years, making a total of nearly 40 per cent of the population who are in, or approaching, the 'third age'[3] Nearly one in eight of the population suffers from a long-term, limiting illness and unemployment rates for men and women are the highest in the county.[4] Indicators of personal wealth follow similar trends. Despite nearly three quarters of houses being owned by their occupiers, central heating was lacking in 18.7 per cent of households (compared with 12.2 per cent in the county as a whole); car ownership is lower than in other rural areas in the county; and 63.2 per cent of Fenland households without cars consist of pensioners only.[5]

Further education (FE) colleges are located in Peterborough, Kings Lynn and Wisbech. The secondary school in Ely, the City of Ely Community College, initiated a ground-breaking rural Access course in Ely in 1994 – initially in partnership with the Board of Continuing Education and, from January 1996 (following changes in funding of courses at HE Level 0), with Cambridge Regional College. These centres do not generally undertake off-site outreach work. The Workers' Educational Association (WEA) is a strong force in Fenland, with groups in Chatteris, Ely, Wisbech and March, and an incipient group in Somersham.

The community education system, pioneered by Henry Morris in Cambridgeshire from the 1930s, was based on the secondary schools (community colleges) which have struggled to continue to provide FE to their communities in the face of government cuts.[6] This provision is under threat in places like Whittlesey, Ramsey, March and Chatteris after severe cuts over successive years in the community education budget of the local authority and an increasing emphasis on youth work.

There has been no direct HE provision in the Fenland for many years, apart from that of the Board of Continuing Education. This has traditionally offered weekly day and evening courses along the skirtlands in Peterborough and at Downham Market.

Local barriers to development work

The most significant barrier presented to the project was the defensive culture generated by past and contemporary attitudes towards Fenlanders by outsiders to the region – and towards 'foreigners' by local people. This cultural context was a prism through which development work could potentially be adversely diffracted, and it was essential to take this into account. The project's success stood or fell on its understanding of this sensitive issue, not least because the project would bring into the Fenland people and organisations which were not indigenous.

These modern attitudes to the Fenland have ancient antecedents, and it was essential for the project worker to understand its persistence and pervasiveness. St. Felix expressed an early example of these pejorative sentiments in the eighth century, presenting the Fenland as a metaphor for paganism.[6] Little appeared to have altered by the seventeenth century, when their contemporaries described the inhabitants of the Fenland in much the same terms. They were said to be idle, miserable and wasteful of valuable resources through poor agricultural management and ignorance. The impetus towards draining and the imposition of arable farming was justified with reference to the benefits which 'civilisation' could bring:

> When Bedford's stately Bank, and noble Drain,
> Shall Paralell the Streights of Magellane,
>
> ... Hearts, thick and tough as Hydes, shall feel Remorse,
> And Souls of Sedge shall understand Discourse,
> New hands shall learn to Work, forget to Steal,
> New leggs shall go to Church, new knees shall kneel.
>
> ... when for sordid Clowns,
> And savage Scythians, There succeeds a Race,
> Worthy the Bliss and Genius of the place...[8]

Modern descriptions of Fen people by outsiders show little has changed, and yet this would be unacceptable in descriptions of national or ethnic groups. Readers too may conduct their own experiment by starting a conversation with some such statement as 'I was reading something about the Fenland recently.' Graham Swift's novel *Waterland* echoes widely-held beliefs of a narrow parochial life, where incest and abuse are the norm among people whose social and intellectual skills are visibly impaired by their environment. Mary Chamberlain's *Fenwomen*, which achieved local notoriety for its methods, has ensured that the community she documented has isolated itself from the outside world for fear of again being unjustly and unknowingly exploited for someone else's benefit.[9]

This was probably the most important aspect that development work needed to address, and which – had it been left untouched – would have rendered our work ineffectual. We had to develop the project 'from the ground up' to ensure that it was not and could not be perceived by local people as yet another attempt to 'civilise' a 'backward area.'

The use of oral history

These cultural perceptions, together with the 1991 Census analysis of the Fenland – both underpinned by recent, more generic work on barriers to participation – pointed to the initial strategies adopted by the project in addressing issues of widening participation. The older age-profile of the Fenland population – the target for the project – mirrored McGivney's conclusions that older people tend to have fewer educational qualifications and are less likely to participate. Also that a willingness to participate in CE is often dependent on previous educational experience, socio-economic background and location. 'The evidence implies that ... certain sections of the community tend not to engage in any form of educational activity after leaving school – older adults, less well-educated people in lower social, economic and occupational strata; women with dependent children; ethnic minority groups; and people living in rural areas.' [10] We expected that McGivney's comment, that motivation among older students was less likely to be employment-related, and more likely to be for 'personal satisfaction, self-development, leisure purposes and family or role transitions', would also be borne out.[11]

We therefore needed an overarching theme for the project that would justify it from the students' as well as HEFCE's perspectives. It needed to validate students' experience, both as older students and as Fenlanders, and to place them on a relatively equal footing with the project, so that they had as much to offer as to gain. We needed to find a non-threatening theme that would appeal to self-interest among a wide constituency. Accreditation was unlikely to be a major selling point. It was these considerations which generated the choice of oral history as the vehicle both in bidding for and in delivering the project.

Since oral history is the history of personal experience, it is student-centred, building on and valuing both the student's past and his/her perceptions of that past. As all experience in oral history must be equally valued collectively in order to achieve a full range of evidence, it follows that all students should be equally valued. This underlying premise was made explicit and allowed the project to attempt to cut across the divisive parameters of social class, education and economic status. By placing a value on students' own experience, we hoped to avoid or ameliorate some of the anxieties and distrust between outsiders and insiders, since each group had something significant to say about their experience of the region.[12]

As an andragogical tool, we felt that oral history exemplified some of the best tenets of adult CE. It is inclusive, builds on students' own experience and allows students to expand their personal and academic confidence in a supportive environment.

Delivery of the project

Careful preparation was essential and focussed on two time-consuming and expensive areas. The first was publicity and the second was ensuring that the project met local needs within the cultural context described above.

Publicity was initially addressed through writing to, visiting and talking to every conceivable local organisation. These included Age Concern; Cambridgeshire Social Services; Community Education organisers; Women's Institutes; Royal British Legion, local societies (everything from local history to gardening); Mothers Unions; and churches. We told them about our plans and asked for comments. The most frequently mentioned was that of cost. Although courses were only £14 for ten weeks in year one – substantially below the Board's concessionary fees for those on state benefits – there was a wide perception that potential students might find it difficult to pay the whole fee at once. Ideally, it should be possible to allow students to pay by instalment, but this required resources far beyond those available within the project.

Fliers, posters and leaflets were sent to all local organisations, local shops, post offices, libraries, museums, health centres and religious organisations. Advertising was placed in every parish magazine, newspaper press releases issued and radio interviews about the project given.

Publicity was carried out in two or three tranches, depending on the time-frame. For example, for courses beginning in late September, initial information fliers were sent out and notices inserted in parish magazines at the beginning of July; in the middle of August more detailed fliers and application forms were distributed; and the same material was distributed again at the beginning of September, together with further, more detailed notices in parish magazines.

The second crucial aspect of preparing for delivery was the staff development of the four local history tutors who were to deliver the first year's courses, and the collection of oral history at each new centre. The project needed to imbue these tutors with its egalitarian ethos, as well as train them in the discipline of oral history. This was done through group meetings and a seminar with an experienced oral historian, as well as meetings and discussions with individual tutors. Paul Thompson's *The Voice of the Past* was used to induct tutors into an understanding of oral history and its methodology.[13]

A rolling programme of short ten-week courses was planned. The initial five weeks of each of the first courses at each centre were delivered at HE Level 0 and were not accredited. The following five weeks were delivered at HE Level 1 and, since outcomes were measured on the basis of the second five weeks learning and activity, accreditation was possible. The achievement of the outcomes was encouraged by the participation of students in recording and transcribing reminiscence; small and whole group discussions within the class; provision of a class bookbox; and the promise of the publication of edited reminiscences in a booklet for each centre.

All courses were provided in daytime, particularly in the mornings when public transport was more frequent and when darkness was not an inhibition to attendance. Central, accessible venues were chosen which offered provision across the whole region. The concentration of population in the Fenland made Ely, March and Wisbech obvious choices. Criteria for venues were that they should not normally be associated with education,[14] they should have easy access to the centre of the settlement, and should have an affordable hourly rental. At Ely, the local Methodist Church Hall provided an ideal, modern environment; at March, the March and District Museum allowed the use of their exhibition rooms; and at Wisbech, the Angles Theatre, and later the Wisbech and Fenland Museum, provided good access for students.

Low student fees, partly underwritten by the funding, were also important. In the first year of the project, fees were set at a flat rate of £14 for ten weeks. We were aware that this was still a substantial sum for students on pensions or state benefits, but decided on this route because of the need for embedding (one of the criteria of the funding) and the lack of the opportunity for remission of student fees. Fees were raised by £2 during each year of the project to reach a flat-rate fee of £18 per ten-week term in 1998–9, which compared favourably with fees charged at the long-established centres at Downham Market and Peterborough College of Adult Education. From 1999–2000 courses at March and Wisbech were locally organised through the respective museums and set their own fees, with only Ely still administered through the Board.

Progression was encouraged through careful planning of subsequent courses, beginning with local and family history in the second year of the project and then continuing to broaden out the subject range (although local history and archaeology remain the most popular subjects). In 1999–2000 centres offered the following courses: 'A History of Parks and Gardens' followed by 'The Archaeology of Fenland Towns' at Ely; 'The Prehistoric Archaeology of Fenland' followed by 'Victorian Social History' at March; and 'The Prehistoric Archaeology of Fenland' and 'The Wash Ports 1000–2000' at Wisbech.

Outcomes

The FOHP can claim some modest success. The funding of £3,716 per year over four years was one of the smallest HEFCE widening-participation awards to HEIs and yet it reaped good rewards. Over four years the project enrolled 592 students on 25 courses, with an average of 23.6 students per course (we had bid for 15 students per course). The project bid for three full-time equivalent students (FTEs) – based on number of contact hours – each year, that is, for 12 FTEs over the funding period. In fact it delivered 27 FTEs over those four years, demonstrating how much can be achieved with relatively small amounts of funding.

Successful centres were established at Ely, March and Wisbech. All three centres were able to sustain enrolments in the second term of each academic year, when student numbers traditionally fall (Table 1). The numbers of students on accredited courses has grown year on year, and by the end of the project these new centres had all been embedded in the Board's conventional provision.

Table 1. Fenland Project: enrolments 1995–99[1]

	Ely[2]	March	Wisbech	Total enrolments[3]
1995–6	23	9	16	48
1996–7				
Autumn	23	27	17	
	51			
Spring	40			
				158 (107)
1997–8				
Autumn	21	22	12	
	57			
Spring	24	19	26	
				181 (124)
1998–9				
Autumn	21	15	37	
	30			
Spring	27	20	24	
				174 (144)

[1] These figures exclude 11 students from Chatteris in 1995–6 and 12 students from Outwell in 1996–7 and in 1997–8.

[2] Italicised figures represent enrolments for non-accredited courses of monthly lectures of nine hours per course.

[3] The figures in brackets represent students attending accredited weekly courses of twenty hours per course.

Table 2. Fenland Project: date of birth by gender (percentages)

Date of birth	Women (n=177)	Men (n=77)
1929 or before	25.4	45.4
1930–1934	20.9	18.1
1935–1939	16.3	19.4
1940–1944	15.8	9.0
1945–1949	9.6	2.0
1950–1954	3.9	2.0
1955 or later	7.9	2.0

FOHP's aim of reaching groups likely to be non-participant targeted women in particular.[15] It succeeded in achieving this, with 70.3 per cent of the students being female, and performed according to the norm in local authority adult education. For example, in Dorset in 1997, 74 per cent of all students aged over 50 years were women.[16]

The project also aimed to reach older learners. Both McGivney and the Carnegie Inquiry[17] had identified this group as less likely to participate in education, although in the Fenland they represent a substantial proportion of the population. Table 2 shows the gender and date of birth of the project students; it relates to individuals (and not enrolments) and excludes the 16 women and 17 men whose ages were not known. The table reveals that the largest group of students were aged over 70 years. This is particularly marked in the case of men; it suggests that retired men are more likely participate in adult education once they become too infirm for other activities.

For both men and women, students born before 1944 (over 45 years of age) form the substantial majority. Both figures are significantly larger than the 38.1 per cent of Fenlanders in this category and the project succeeded in reaching older learners in general, and women in particular. The success of the project can be compared against the proportion of older students in part-time HE in general, where, for example, 17 per cent of Open University students are over 50 years of age, while in other institutions 'learners over 50 years of age are a minority.'[18]

We were interested to measure the educational qualifications of older students who attended the project's courses. As Table 3 demonstrates, the project succeeded in its aim of widening participation since a significant number of students either had no qualifications or only O-levels. The number of students, particularly women, born before 1934 who did not list their previous educational achievement was notable. Evidence from the oral history project showed that many older women had left school without qualifications at the age of 14 to go into work. This was confirmed by the findings of other researchers, showing the high proportions of older men and women who had no qualifications.[19] Those born after 1934 were more likely to have been positively affected by the educational reforms of the immediate post-war period. The project concluded intuitively that those women born before 1934, whose educational qualifications were 'not known', probably included a high percentage with no qualifications who felt stigmatised by the answer. The numbers in this group fell sharply as students became younger.

Table 3. Fenland Project: educational attainment by gender (percentages)

Highest educational attainment	Women (n=223)	Men (n=94)
Not known	30.4	29.7
None	8.5	14.8
O-level	16.5	13.8
A-level	6.7	3.1
Professional qualification	21.9	21.2
Degree	9.8	10.6
Higher degree	5.3	6.3

Since one of the aims of the project was to encourage previous non-participants in HE, we were interested to see how many people had studied with the Board before. The results are not quite as conclusive as we would have liked but are nevertheless encouraging. The student enrolment form, which was used to collect the data, asked two questions: 'Have you studied with the Board of Continuing Education before?' and 'Have you studied in higher education before?' Many students when first enrolling answered 'no' to the first question and left the second question blank. When they enrolled on subsequent courses, they answered 'yes' to both questions, which was accurate since the Board does offer HE. Table 4 is therefore compiled on the basis of information given at the time of individual students' first enrolment with the Board.

Table 4. Fenland Project: previous experience of studying with the Board of Continuing Education

Educational achievement	No	Yes	Not known
None	21	6	4
O-level	35	9	6
A-level	5	7	0
Professional qualification	43	15	11
Degree	13	15	4
Higher degree	11	3	5
No response	15	12	77
Total	143	67	107

It is further broken down according to the students' previous educational achievements. We wished to be sure we had attracted previous non-participants, rather than those with varied educational backgrounds who were already part of the Board's cohort. Again, FOHP has been successful on this count. As before, there were intuitive reasons for suspecting that a significant proportion of those who did not answer the first question had not previously studied with the Board. They clearly included the large number of older women who did not wish to list their previous educational achievement.

One of the criteria used to embed the project into the Board's conventional provision was credit award. Students who achieved credit could be seen to have progressed into conventional CE. Table 5 shows that credit was awarded to 59 per cent of those women (106/176) and 46 per cent (37/79) of those men who studied on accredited courses within the project. The non-accredited monthly lecture programme at Ely was used to test the extent to which accreditation was an issue among students. Since just 17 per cent attended only these non-accredited courses we could not conclude that the recognition of learning through credit was irrelevant to our students, whatever their age.

Table 5. Fenland Project: students achieving credit by gender

	Women (n=223)	Men (n=94)
Credit awarded	106	37
Certificate of Achievement	6	2
Credit not awarded	64	40
Results not yet known	3	2
Non-accredited courses	44	13

A second criterion for embedding and for increased participation was the retention of students on subsequent courses. Table 6 shows that a significant percentage of students did re-enrol. These figures are rather coarse and need further analysis; only 48 students (those who enrolled in year one) had the opportunity of taking all courses at their centre, and the numbers steadily increased as the project progressed.

Table 6. Fenland Project: students progressing within the Board

Progression to other courses with the Board	Women	Men
None	133	65
2 courses	42	16
3 courses	22	4
4 courses	8	3
5 or more courses	18	6
Percentage progressing	40.3	30.8

On many counts, therefore, the project appeared to have succeeded. Its project-specific results can be measured against national conclusions; for example, that 'few older people participate, especially among those who have completed their initial education before the age of 16' or that 'participation is even less by older women.'[20]

The project also had visible outcomes as far as the students were concerned. It published three booklets based on the oral histories of three centres: *The Light of Other Days: Oral History from Wisbech*; *Half in Sunlight, Half in Shade: Oral History from Outwell and March*; and *Portrait of the Fens: Oral History from Ely*. The first two booklets were edited by the tutor, and the third by the tutor in combination with an editorial group drawn from the class. The booklets were illustrated with personal and archive photographs, and were thematically organised in chapters, including 'Family', 'Work', 'Schooling' and 'Community'. Each participant in the course received a free copy and was invited to a reception held at the Board (and attended by HEFCE) to launch the booklets in May 1999, to which free travel was provided.

There were also some unexpected outcomes. At Ely, a group of students from the oral history class who were interested in local history, set themselves up as a small research group that undertook projects under the Board's direction. This group published their final projects themselves as *Ely Remembered*. At March, students inspired by a local history course, following the initial course, have collated and published a booklet on the local history of the town, *From Mercheford to March*, with the Board's support.

The small amount of funding for the project meant that there were four areas of concern that we did not have the resources to address. First, we were aware that there were students for whom removable barriers still existed; in particular those with transport needs (either as a result of distance or infirmity) and those carers for whom there was no other caring provision. Although more funding would have allowed the project to begin to address these issues, other significant questions emerged. Universities are not usually able to overcome these kinds of barriers without some kind of special funding; perhaps greater collaboration between government agencies and HE institutions is needed.

Second, guidance was an important issue that did not receive specialised attention. We would have liked to have been able to provide ongoing pre-course and on-course guidance for students through a peripatetic guidance worker. This guidance work should include questions of student study-skill support, with its own implications for the curriculum.

Third, it soon became apparent that experienced adult teachers were far more effective in delivering the specialised aims of the project (however patchy their knowledge of local history) than experienced local historians with little expertise in teaching adults. The least successful class was at Chatteris where the tutor, a museum curator with no previous teaching experience, was more interested in collecting the memories of older local students than in using oral history as a teaching tool. Specific staff development in oral history, and in inculcating the ethos of the project, was undertaken but was more time-consuming and expensive. To our regret, it was not extensive enough to change the underlying perceptions of this tutor. More funding would make a substantial difference.

Finally, measurement of the success of FOHP has raised many qualitative issues that a raw analysis of the Higher Education Statistical Agency (HESA) data has not been able to answer. As described below, the HESA results appear to show greater inclusiveness between locals and foreigners, and increased participation from older students with low educational attainment. Qualitative research is needed to explore the extent to which these intuitive conclusions can be supported.

On the other hand, this start-up funding has allowed the Board to undertake developmental work that it might not otherwise have been able to afford. The benefits to the Fenland have been substantial. Where no courses in HE were previously offered, courses are now available throughout the area, augmenting the centres that had previously been established around the edge of the Fen Basin at Ramsey, Peterborough and Downham Market.

Conclusion

We have learned a great deal from the Fenland Oral History Project. It has achieved the aims of widening participation in terms of the gender, age and previous educational achievement of its students. A substantial number of students have achieved recognition for their learning through credit, while a significant percentage have continued to study with the Board.

We have also learned much about the time-consuming nature of development work, whose slower pace is essential for good networking (the project was able to fund about thirty days' work each year for the project worker); about the need to consult with local communities about their needs and wants, and about the ways in which local networks work; about the expense of development in widened participation (the issues of student payments and guidance are good examples); about the needs of previously non-participant students; and, in particular, the necessity for guidance about progression and about study skills.

The project has highlighted important issues concerning the nature of lifelong learning and its implications for older and poorer students. Much discussion has emphasised the vocational nature of learning and the necessity for workers to re-skill or upgrade their skills. This interpretation may not always be to the advantage of older students, particularly those who are unlikely to re-enter the workforce.

Conversely, the transformative power of adult FE, particularly in the liberal arts, cannot be denied. It empowers students through changing their perceptions of themselves and in giving them access to skills which allow them to take a greater control of their lives. The project's success in addressing cultural perceptions was, we felt, demonstrated in the relatively large number of older, formerly non-participant students with low previous educational achievement, and in their continuing progression in HE with the Board. Students' intense pride in their locality and local culture was given expression in the booklets, conferring physical value to the project's aims. These publications were an essential part of the process, since it was only through them that the project demonstrated its commitment to the students.

Economic arguments suggest that a modest investment in adult CE would reap disproportionate benefits in terms of retaining the physical and mental mobility of older students; the health of poorer students may also be improved. Yet economic arguments are themselves a travesty. The 'Gradgrind' approach to education needs to be decisively rejected. The potential exclusion of older and poorer students from CE, if accreditation and vocationalism are to be the mainsprings of future 'lifelong' learning, reveals a fundamental and serious misapprehension about the meaning and value of education.

Most importantly, we have learned that unless it is grounded both within local culture and within an androgogical framework, development work in adult CE and FE may be fatally flawed from the outset.

Notes

1.   Research Group, Cambridgeshire County Council (1993). *1991 Census – The Local Picture. Fenland Report*. Cambridgeshire County Council; p. 3.
2.   *Ibid.*, p. 5.
3.   *Ibid.*, p. 22.
4.   *Ibid.*, p. 8.
5.   *Ibid.*, pp. 12–15.
6.   See Chapter 4.
7.   St. Felix wrote: '[the fen] was of immense size [with] ... immense marshes, now a black pool of water, now foul-running streams. ... [There was] an island especially obscure, which oft-times many men had attempted to inhabit, but no man could do it on account of the manifold horrors and fears, and the loneliness of the wide wilderness.' Quoted in Darby, H.C. (1974). *The Medieval Fenland*. Cambridge University Press.
8.   Said to be composed by Samuel Fortrey (1685). The History or Narrative of the Great Level of the Fenns Called Bedford Level. Quoted in *Fenland Notes and Queries*; (1889) vol. 1: p. 322.
9.   Swift, G. (1983). *Waterland*. Heineman; Chamberlain, M. (1977). *Fenwomen*. Virago.
10.   McGivney, V. (1993). Participation and non-participation: a review of the literature. In Edwards, R., Sieminski, S. and Zeldin, D. eds. *Adult Learners, Education and Training*. Routledge.
11.   *Ibid.*, pp. 14–15 and p. 24.
12.   An enormous amount of work in and on oral history has been published in recent years. Thompson, P. (1978). *The Voice of the Past* (Oxford University Press) is still one of the most masterly, but many others can be found, for example, through the National Sound Archive, the Oral History Society and at the University of Sussex.
13.   *Ibid.*
14.   McGivney, *op. cit.*, pp. 19–20, had noted that 'people who have ostensibly "failed" in the school system do not wish to repeat that failure. Many are consequently suspicious of education in any form.' By removing the project from schools we hoped to reinforce the message that the experience we offered would be different.
15.   Tables 2–6 are based on information for individual students and not on total enrolments: 275 of the project's total of 592 enrolments were repeats.
16.   Carlton, S. and Soulsby, J. (1999). *Learning To Grow Older and Bolder*. NIACE; p. 34.
17.   The Carnegie United Kingdom Trust (1993). *The Carnegie Inquiry into the Third Age: Life, Work and Livelihood in the Third Age*. Table 6.3: p. 139, shows 45 per cent of all students were in the third age. The percentage participating drops sharply from 24 per cent aged 45 to 54 to nine per cent aged over 65.

18. Carlton and Soulsby, *op. cit.*, p. 46.
19. McGivney, *op. cit.*, pp. 14–15; Carlton and Soulsby, *op. cit.*, p. 24: 43 per cent of those aged 55 to 64 in 1997 had no qualifications; Carnegie Inquiry, *op. cit.*, Chart 6.1: p. 138, shows similar figures.
20. Carlton and Soulsby, *op. cit.*, p. 30.

11

The University of the Highlands and Islands project: a rural curriculum delivered remotely

Jane Plenderleith and Veronica Adamson[1]

Introduction: background and locality

The Highlands and Islands of Scotland is a remote and rugged area on the periphery of both Britain and Europe. Situated in the north-western extremities of the British Isles, the region has struggled against the adversities of geographic, economic and social isolation, and has suffered severely in terms of economic decline and depopulation. The area comprises nearly 20 per cent of the land mass of Britain, but has less than one per cent of the UK population (fewer than half a million inhabitants) and, as such, is one of the least densely populated areas of Europe. With the exception of the conurbation of Inverness, which is one of Europe's fastest-growing cities, most of the inhabitants live in small and widely-dispersed towns and villages. At the time of the 1991 Census there were 93 inhabited islands of the Shetland and Orkney archipelagos, and the Inner and Outer Hebrides.

The region has long suffered from a lack of critical mass to support services and facilities, inexorably exacerbated by concomitant emigration and population decline. In the nineteenth century, communities were forcibly moved to make way for sheep. In the twentieth century, traditional micro-industries such as fishing and farming were eroded in the face of strong national and international competition. Many of the region's young people have sought education and careers outside the Highlands and Islands, particularly those seeking higher education (HE) opportunities. Indeed, historically, a significantly high proportion of the region's youth has entered HE. During the early 1980s, when 14 per cent of school-leavers in England were entering HE, and the figure for Scotland as a whole was 21 per cent, the percentage figure for the Highlands and Islands was a staggering 32 per cent.[2]

However, all of the current 22 universities and HE institutions in Scotland lie in or close to the more densely populated triangle formed by the cities of Aberdeen, Edinburgh and Glasgow. Young people in search of a university education had to leave and, once departed, they seldom returned.

The idea that the Highlands and Islands of Scotland deserve a university of their own is not a new one. Sir Thomas Urquhart published his plans for higher education of the young men of Cromarty as early as 1653.[3] In a paper headed *On Education* and probably dated around 1706, Sir George Mackenzie, First Earl of Cromartie, put forward his own proposals for a proto-university based in Inverness. The curriculum was to include instruction for women in morality, and weekly 'publick lessons', perhaps an early example of adult continuing education (CE).[4] More recently, another bid for Inverness under the 1964 Robbins expansion failed in the face of competition from Stirling; to the dismay of many outside the central belt, Scotland's newest university of the time was established close to all the others.

In 1992, the year when the Further and Higher Education (Scotland) Act brought the total of Scotland's Higher Education Institutions to the present 22, Sir Graham Hills (former Principal and Vice Chancellor of the University of Strathclyde in Glasgow) proposed to the then Highland Regional Council a model university, based on a multi-campus partnership of local institutions. The blueprint was for a university that would be regional in terms of being both in and of its region.[5]

Hills cites the transportation revolution and, in particular, the information revolution as primary factors in the call from many remote areas in Europe for HE opportunities to be available *in situ*. Of course, as the figures above indicate, significant proportions of the Highlands and Islands populace have taken up HE opportunities outside the region. Current participation in Open University programmes of study by adult learners within the area is also high. That said, the economic arguments for an established university in, and of, the area are considerable. As an industry in its own right, HE is generally sound business; in terms of inward investment, a university functions as a significant economic multiplier.

One of the most significant and far-reaching aspects of the Hills vision was the new learning paradigm it proposed for HE in the Highlands and Islands. Drawing on *The New Production of Knowledge* (Gibbons *et al.*),[6] Hills advocated the alternative 'mode 2' basis for undergraduate education. Broadly, this approach to HE is transferable skills-based rather than specific knowledge-based, and aims to equip graduates with the abilities and attributes required to function in a variety of employment situations. For Hills, 'mode 2' as a learning mode, as opposed to 'mode 1' as a teaching mode, was to be the defining pedagogical impetus behind the new university in the move towards a 'learning society'.[7]

The project

In 1993, Highlands and Islands Enterprise established the University of the Highlands and Islands (UHI) project, charged with the task of establishing a university in and for the Highlands and Islands of Scotland. It was indeed to be a new university for the twenty-first century, a collegiate federation linked by a powerful information and communications highway. Its pedagogical approach was not to be based on distance learning modes and models, since the Open

University and outreach ventures from existing universities were already seen to be catering for these needs. The fundamental concept of UHI was that individuals should be able to engage locally in learning despite their distant location; that people and places should be linked in community learning networks, operating collectively as a single university entity; and that the curriculum should be tailored specifically to the economic and social needs and aspirations of the area.

At the time of writing, UHI is a federation of 13 institutions of FE and HE. It includes local authority-operated colleges (such as Orkney and Shetland Colleges); larger incorporated FE colleges such as Inverness, Perth and Moray Colleges; industry-funded institutions like the North Atlantic Fisheries College; specialist colleges such as the Sabhal Mòr Ostaig Gaelic College on Skye and the Highland Theological College; and two research institutions – the Scottish Association for Marine Science near Oban and Seafish Aquaculture on Ardnamurchan.

Provision exists and negotiations are underway for the addition of new partners: Lochaber College at Fort William and the Highland Psychiatric Research Foundation, based at Inverness, currently hold UHI Associate Partner status. Many of these academic partners in UHI also operate local networks of learning centres, making provision available to small and geographically dispersed communities. The recent securing of significant European funding will facilitate a strategic and consolidated approach to community learning networks across the area.

UHI's development trajectory has been steep and swift. In the autumn of 1996, the Millennium Commission awarded £33.35 million to the UHI project, one of the largest single awards in Scotland. This funding was primarily for the physical infrastructure of the emerging university and includes a number of campus-based estate projects, plus the establishment of a pan-Highlands and Islands wide area network (WAN) for information and communications technology (ICT). This broadband network will carry a number of services, including data transfer, telephony, video conferencing and digital broadcasting. It provides a technological platform for delivering the curriculum to the communities served by UHI; links the partner institutions and community centres within a region-wide educational and communications network; and offers the region online access to the databases and information sources of the world. Crucially, ICT provides a platform for overcoming the obstacles of space, distance and dispersal that had previously defined and determined educational and social developments in the Highlands and Islands.

In 1998, UHI published its first *Strategic Planning Framework* for the period 1998–2001. The stated UHI mission is: 'To establish for the Highlands and Islands of Scotland a collegiate university which will reach the highest standards and play a pivotal role in our educational, social and cultural development.'[8] Commitment to the region's unique culture and heritage is paramount, as is a response to the specific economic and social needs of the area in general, and its very different

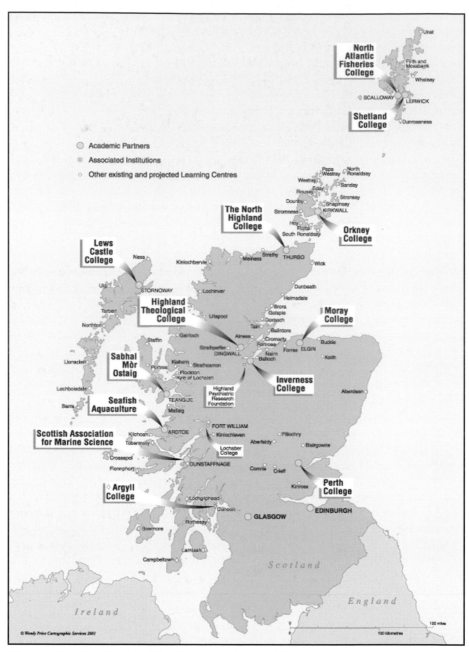

Figure 1. The UHI Millenium Institute 2001

constituent communities, mediated and transmitted through ICT. Put more succinctly, the needs of the communities drive the curriculum, and these together drive the technology through which the curriculum is made available.

Also in 1998, UHI achieved the significant step of accreditation by the Open University Validation Services (OUVS) for the awards it was developing. The embryonic university was on the way to providing relevant, quality HE and learning opportunities for and in the Highlands and Islands. Steps were evidently being taken towards the realisation of Hills' vision of a university in and of its region.

The lifelong learning agenda is of vital importance for UHI in its commitment to making HE available to all communities throughout the region. The 1998 Fryer Report, *Learning for the Twenty-First Century*, set the scene for lifelong learning in the UK context and that of Europe. [9] Fryer determined the agenda for lifelong learning by identifying it as an essential element in tackling social exclusion, the single most significant agent for change in the move towards a twenty-first century 'knowledge economy'.

In the Scottish context, the publication of *Opportunity Scotland: a paper on lifelong learning* was particularly significant for UHI.[10] This report was the Scottish version of the English government Green Paper *The Learning Age* and it specifically mentions the University of the Highlands and Islands project and the government's support for the emerging university. This is of course especially pertinent in the context of the recent inauguration of the first parliament on Scottish soil for nearly three hundred years, with a strong educational agenda and commitment. The UHI project supports the key themes of *Opportunity Scotland*, namely: 'raising awareness'; 'improving access'; 'extending participation and tackling exclusion'; 'encouraging progression'; and 'ensuring quality'.[11] These are clearly significant factors in the realisation of the positive socio-cultural as well as socio-economic benefits of HE, and indicate UHI's potential to facilitate the achievement of the key deliverables for the government and the Scottish Executive of economic competitiveness and social inclusion.

In December 1998 the UHI project reached another significant milestone in the submission of a formal request to the Secretary of State for Scotland to be designated an HE institution. The Scottish Office has subsequently conducted a formal sectoral consultation exercise, and asked the Quality Assurance Agency for Higher Education (QAA) in Scotland to conduct an audit visit of the project and the academic partners in autumn 1999. A formal response from the new Scottish Parliament to the request for designation is anticipated in the course of the year 2000. If positive, the next milestone objective will be to meet the emerging QAA criteria for degree-awarding powers.

It is worth pausing here to note the comparative speed of these developments. From the time of the initial conception of a university for the Highlands and Islands of Scotland to the establishment of the UHI Project Office, almost four hundred years have elapsed. The project is charged with establishing a designated HE institution within four years – a tall order by anyone's standards.

Clearly, achieving the vision of a regional university, both in and of its geographical area, requires careful planning in terms of its curriculum content, the methods by which that content will be delivered, and the assurance of quality of the learning experience across the entire spectrum of provision. The disparate nature of the individual partners provides strength in scope, but poses particular challenges in terms of encouraging unity in diversity. Not least, the issues of sustainability and long-term funding require consideration and planning.

Curriculum

The UHI curriculum has been developed through consultation of the subject experts in the academic partners with appropriate community, business and industry interest groups. A number of curriculum development working groups were established in 1997 with a tripartite remit. Their first task was to consider existing staff expertise, resource availability and curriculum provision throughout the network of academic partners. Their next task was to identify gaps in this provision and areas for the further development of a HE curriculum, with due cognisance of student and employer needs, staff expertise and learner support requirements. On the basis of these two activities, their third and final task was the recommendation of the development of provision to fulfil these identified curricular needs, along with identifying the requisite human and material resources. Recent academic restructuring has subsumed these working groups into five new UHI faculties – arts, culture and heritage; business and leisure studies; environmental and natural systems sciences; health and social studies; information and engineering systems – charged with the task, amongst others, of continuing and refining curriculum developments.

In addition to the five faculties, four research schools have been established, and a number of PhD studentships sponsored. This is an ambitious initiative, designed to cultivate and enhance indigenous research and development for the Highlands and Islands. UHI academic staff are also encouraged to engage in programmes of higher study and continuous professional development. It is recognised that a paradigm shift is required by staff already experienced in the design and delivery of FE programmes to the more learner-centred, independent approaches demanded by a HE curriculum and methodology. Significant support accorded to the achievement of this shift.

In accordance with the principles recommended by the Garrick Report for Scotland to the National Committee of Inquiry into Higher Education,[12] UHI has developed a range of broad-based, three-year bachelors degrees (Scottish ordinary degrees) with a vocational emphasis. While the UHI Academic Council has recently agreed in principle the development of selected honours provision across a range of curriculum areas, these developments are on hold pending a track record of quality delivery. By September 1998, nine degree awards had been validated under the aegis of the aforementioned UHI/OUVS accreditation agreement. By September 1999, a further eight awards had been added, including the first taught postgraduate award. The UHI project also inherited some existing HE provision that had been validated by other Scottish HEIs for delivery by some UHI academic partners. Developments continue apace: a further 14 undergraduate and postgraduate awards are currently in preparation for the admission of students in 2000 and 2001. An important element in UHI's curriculum developments at present is the integration of existing Higher National Certificate and Diploma awards into a unifying curriculum structure and quality assurance procedures. The keynote is diversity in unity. The entry for UHI that appears in the Universities Central Admissions Service (UCAS) Handbook for Entry 2001 lists more than 100 full-time undergraduate awards available across the academic partners and within the communities they serve.

The degree awards developed by UHI reflect the intention to establish high-quality HE provision for the region and to tailor this provision specifically to the region's needs. Developments in business administration, for example, place significant emphasis on the small- and medium-sized enterprises that constitute the vast majority of active businesses in the area. ICT is an important and integrated curriculum focus, as well as a means of facilitating its delivery. The acquisition of transferable skills is recognised as vitally important for businesses that rely on all-rounders rather than specialists.

Applied science developments in fisheries, land management, forestry and marine ecology are all designed to meet specific industry-orientated economic needs. Sustainable development, rurality and environmental management are recurrent themes in the UHI curriculum. Provision in tourism, leisure and hospitality management addresses issues particular to the Highlands and Islands in the context of generic industry and commercial needs, concerns and policies.

There are substantial collaborative curriculum ventures with Scandinavia, the Arctic and the North Atlantic Rim, where common issues of isolation, rurality and sustainability are paramount. The importance of the transferable skills required by the lifelong learner in the economic marketplace of the twenty-first century is reflected in the formal integration of personal and professional capabilities into all modules and programmes of the UHI undergraduate curriculum.

Delivery

Much deliberation and analysis has taken place with regard to the delivery of the UHI curriculum. The need to deliver courses of learning to a variety of learners in a range of settings is fundamental. There is a plethora of learning centres across the area, ranging from college-based learning resource centres to community-based, multi-purpose meeting places. These learning centres have different names, different types of owner, ranges of uses and funding mechanisms. Currently there are approximately 50 learning centres, operated largely by the academic partners, offering a range of provision in a variety of ways. One of the current developmental imperatives for UHI is the mapping of these centres and the activities they may support, and the establishment of a baseline quality threshold for learners across the region.

Embedded in the basic definition of a learning centre, as a place where individuals can go to engage in learning, are certain assumptions that may be expressed as 'learner entitlements'. These include access to a computer with a connection to the UHI WAN; access to a subject tutor and a student adviser; access to materials; and access to a learning space. Whatever the mode of delivery, the learning experience depends on resources. A common definition of a learning resource would generally refer to the way in which the content is packaged – such as in print, CD-ROM or audio-visual format. However, in the context of UHI and networked learning, a wider categorisation of a learning resource is proposed; one that takes into consideration the mutual interdependence of the human, material and environmental resources required for meaningful community learning. In January 1999, the UHI learning and environmental technologies working group under the leadership of Professor Alistair Macfarlane published its report *Towards a Learning Strategy for the University of the Highlands and Islands*, referred to internally as the LET Report.[13] This has proved an important document for staff across the network engaged in developing a HE curriculum for networked delivery, and allows an insight into the kind of learning strategies and methodologies that are envisaged for the emerging university.

Issues

There is, then, considerable evidence not only of the need for a university in and for the Highlands and Islands of Scotland, but also of the successes to date of the UHI project and the federal academic partners in working towards this goal. There are also significant challenges to overcome in a number of key areas.

Already there is evidence of UHI's success in addressing the needs of the lifelong learner in the Highlands and Islands. According to 1997 statistics, UHI academic partners were successfully providing a locally-developed community curriculum to a student population of almost 6,000 students, of whom around half are part-time learners.[14] In terms of equality of educational opportunity, there is a near equity in male/female balance, more than 50 per cent of learners are aged over 25 and over 80 per cent are local to their academic partner institution. These are early, positive indicators that UHI is addressing the issues of social exclusion and geographical isolation in a context of lifelong learning.

However, little concrete evidence is available to date of the extent to which UHI is meeting the higher educational needs of all its constituents from all sectors of the community. This is particularly relevant in the context of ethnic minority groupings, about which much remains to be learned in the area. The 1991 Census indicated a significant ethnic minority population in the Highlands and Islands, but, at present, scant information is available as to potential under-representation in HE participation. A highly sophisticated 'equal opportunities policy' has recently been developed for UHI. If successfully implemented, this detailed policy, compiled through consultation with recognised experts from a wide spectrum of interest groups, should lay a foundation for equality of representation for all social and ethnic groupings in the HE community of the Highlands and Islands.

In February 1999, UHI launched its unique 'linguistic and cultural identity policy' which pledged to give equal weight and import to five indigenous 'languages' of the Highlands and Islands, and the different cultural groupings they represent. These 'languages' are English, Gaelic, Orcadian, Scots and Shetlandic. UHI recognises English and Gaelic as formal languages for curriculum delivery and assessment. Sabhal Mòr Ostaig College on Skye conducts all its business through the medium of Gaelic, and significant proportions of the curriculum at other academic partners are delivered and assessed in Gaelic. The UHI library management system, a uniquely distributed system that has unified the disparate catalogues of all the academic partners in the federation, has a bilingual English/Gaelic web interface. The other 'languages' identified in the UHI linguistic and cultural identity policy are not currently recognised in the library management system, nor in quality assurance and academic management procedures.

The issues of long-term recurrent funding, the sustainability of curriculum developments and delivery modes and methods are plainly crucial for the future of the project. Student uptake of the HE curriculum is mainly at Levels 1 and 2 (HNC and HND), with few students currently engaged on degree-level programmes. Significant sums of money have been invested in the development of relevant and accessible programmes of study, in terms of curriculum content, quality assurance systems and structures, staff development and learning resource provision. A return on this investment, in terms of student recruitment, enhanced employment opportunities and economic improvement, is plainly required. While efforts are being made to encourage new student recruits and existing student progression, some further research may be required to identify and address issues affecting degree-level engagement.

There is a clear need for enhanced local, national and international recruitment and awareness-raising strategies. The recruitment ethos of UHI is emphatically to provide choice for potential students. While substantial numbers of the region's youth may continue to migrate to study, the option to remain within the region is now available. It is anticipated that the UHI student base will increasingly contain part-time learners and mature students. There are evident implications here for both the curriculum and its delivery. A UHI course information line, established in November 1998, takes increasing numbers of calls from members of the public, usually in response to regional advertising campaigns. The majority of these calls are from interested parties, impatiently awaiting the delivery of the provision they want at a locality near their home. Whilst there is tremendous public support for the concept of a university in and for the Highlands and Islands, there is understandably little public conception of the wider issues, such as viability and availability of resources. There are also significant challenges posed in encouraging public engagement with the notion that university learning is not necessarily contingent on grand open courtyards and lofty Gothic spires, but can in fact take place in the village hall, public library or primary school.

A further challenge for the near future is the achievement of the aims set, and the methodologies proposed, in the LET Report.[15] Efforts will now focus on the establishment and monitoring of community learning networks; the development and implementation of the resources and environments they require; the learning activities that will take place; and the impact of the centres and the learning on the communities and the learners themselves. UHI has formed strategic alliances with other providers currently involved in the delivery of HE to the Highlands and Islands; for example, the universities of Aberdeen and Heriot-Watt and the Open University. Credit-mapping exercises and joint curriculum developments are underway. It is to be hoped that the interests of the students and communities of the region will prevail in the meaningful research into the most effective matching of individual learners with content, mode and learning media. It is further to be hoped that the 'mode 2' learning strategies favoured by early curriculum planners in UHI, will not only come into force through the activities of curriculum developers and deliverers, but will find favour with employers and provide the anticipated economic impetus.

Student feedback from the 1998–9 academic session indicated that while ICT was recognised as an important and integral part of the UHI curriculum and its delivery, some assumptions had been made about the propensity of all students, particularly mature learners, to acquire the necessary ICT skills with sufficient speed and alacrity. It is an established tenet of educational hermeneutics that the human mind thinks with ideas, not with information.[16, 17] Education is both a social and a cognitive process,[18] and there are clear dangers inherent in basing the use of computers in education on an outmoded view of human beings as information processors. For meaningful learning, experience and ideas must be privileged over technologised knowledge. UHI is striving to remain true to the principle that the communities choose the curriculum and that these two together determine the appropriate technology. Communities should be able to decide the curriculum that is relevant for them on the basis of needs and wants, not availability of materials or expertise. This in turn raises issues of ownership, responsibility and funding.

The complexity of the UHI federal structure necessitates complex administrative and academic management structures. These are designed to promote for meaningful debate and to ensure that the views of all stakeholders are ably represented in the emergence of the new university. The integration of universities with regional development is most readily achieved not by top-down planning mechanisms, but by ensuring that all the various interested parties – education and training providers, employers, trade unions, labour market agencies and learners – have an understanding of one another's roles and the factors encouraging or inhibiting regional engagement.[19]

In her analysis of post-Dearing academic management structures, Susan Weil offers the following telling comment on the pitfalls of complex committee structures:

> *Within the formal system of universities, committees lumber on, often upholding rigidities and unspoken assumptions, and seldom functioning as sites for a critical scrutiny of the limitations of existing epistemologies of practice.[20]*

However, UHI is perhaps uniquely positioned in the context of British HE to implement the kind of organisational structures that will promote stability in diversity, and the ability to respond swiftly and meaningfully to changing social and economic conditions.

Conclusion and postscript

The people of the Highlands and Islands have waited a long time for 'their university' and they want it *now*. There are two major drives within UHI, with potential for some creative tension in their interaction. These are the drive to take the curriculum to the communities and the drive for degree-awarding powers and university status. The former must not jeopardise the latter; the latter should not stifle the former. Public and sectoral scrutiny of the UHI project is intense, especially in terms of the relevance of the curriculum and the modes and methods of delivery. The courage of conviction is required.

Increasing globalisation of the HE sector and its products poses particular challenges and presents particular opportunities to the Highlands and Islands – not least in developing and delivering a curriculum that is both locally relevant and internationally valid. The announcement by the UK Education Minister, David Blunkett, of support for the Higher Education Funding Council's 'e-university' project gives an indication of the possible shape of HE in the twenty-first century. In December 2000, the First Minister of Scotland visited Inverness to announce the designation of UHI as a HE institution. Whilst not yet conferring university status, designation meant that UHI would receive funding from the Scottish Higher Education Funding Council. Considerable efforts were being exerted in the realisation of a seventeenth-century vision for the new millennium .

On 1 April 2001, the Scottish Parliament declared the legal designation of UHI as a HE institution, with the new name of the UHI Millennium Institute. Six months later, on 1 October 2001, Professor Robert Cormack was appointed Director and Chief Executive of UHI. Widening access to quality HE for the dispersed communities of the Highlands and Islands and facilitating seamless progression between FE and HE were identified as development priorities for the new institution.

The emerging evidence indicates that UHI is beginning to have a significant impact both within and beyond the Highlands and Islands. Research for the

Scottish Higher Education Funding Council,[21] on widening access to HE in Scotland between 1996 and 1998, concludes that 'the most striking change in participation over the two-year period is the increase in students studying in flexible learning modes from the remote areas of the Highlands and Islands.' This development, which perhaps heralds a staunching of the flow of people seeking HE opportunities outside the Highlands and Islands, is most probably related to UHI initiatives. The Scottish Parliament is also interested in the innovative new institution. As an article in *The Higher* in October 2001 noted:

> *... there is increasing interest in blurring the divide between the two sectors [FE and HE] for the benefit of students. The Enterprise and Lifelong Learning Committee is clearly intrigued by the UHI Millennium Institute, the Highlands and Islands' high-tech federation of further education colleges and research institutes that has now won designation as a higher education institution.*[22]

Notes

1.   Any opinions expressed in this case study are those of the authors and do not necessarily reflect the views of the institution. The substantive final draft of this chapter was prepared in May 2000. The UHI website is: http://www.uhi.ac.uk/index.htm

2.   Hills, G. (1997). The University of the Highlands and Islands: Scotland's first regional university. In Crawford, R., ed. *A Future for Scottish Higher Education, Committee of Scottish Higher Education Principals*; pp. 86–96 (quote p. 87).

3.   *Ibid.*, p. 89.

4.   Clough, M. (1990). *Two Houses.* Aberdeen University Press; p. 157f.

5.   Hills, *op. cit.*, p. 86.

6.   Gibbons, M., Limoges, C., Nowotny, H., Schwartzman, S., Scott, P. and Trow, M. (1994). *The New Production of Knowledge.* Sage.

7.   Hills, *op. cit.*, p. 95.

8.   UHI (1998). *Strategic Planning Framework* 1998–2001; p. ii.

9.   National Advisory Group for Continuing Education and Lifelong Learning (1997). *Learning for the Twenty-first Century.* (The Fryer Report), DfEE.

10. Scottish Office (1998). *Opportunity Scotland: a Paper on Lifelong Learning.*

11. *Ibid.*, p. 3.

12. National Committee for Enquiry into Higher Education (1997). *Higher Education in the Learning Society.* (The Dearing Report), HMSO.

13. UHI (1999). *Towards a Learning Strategy for the University of the Highlands and Islands Project.*

14. UHI (1999). *Strategic Plan 1999/2000–2002/2003*; p. 4.

15. UHI, *Towards a Learning Strategy.*

16. Capra, F. (1996). *The Web of Life.* Anchor, Doubleday, New York.

17. Weil, S. (1999). Re-creating universities for 'beyond the stable state':

from 'Dearingesque' systematic control to post-Dearing systemic learning and inquiry. *System Research and Behavioural Science: Special Edition on Dearing and Higher Education*; vol. 16, no. 2: pp. 171–190.

18. Newby, H. (1999). Higher education in the twenty-first century – some possible futures. *Perspectives, Policy and Practice in Higher Education*. vol. 3, no. 4; pp. 106–13, (quote p. 107).

19. Goddard, J.B. (1997). *Universities and Regional Development: An Overview*. University of Newcastle upon Tyne.

20. Weil, *op. cit.*, p. 5.

21. Raab, G.M. and Storkey, H.R. (2001). *Widening Access to Higher Education in Scotland: Evidence for Change from 1996/7 to 1998/99*. Scottish Higher Education Funding Council.

22. *The Higher*. 19 October 2001.

12

Towards a University of the Moors: widening participation in North Yorkshire

Peter Ryley

Introduction

The North York Moors is an area of outstanding natural beauty and includes both high moorland and coastal areas. The coastal towns have a declining fishing industry and growing tourism. Both Scarborough and Whitby are well-established traditional holiday destinations but with changing patterns of usage. With competition from cheap foreign travel, day-trips and long weekends have replaced the traditional one- or two-week stay. The upland areas have prosperous villages and market towns, with statistically successful schools. House prices are buoyant and unemployment is low. Yet the characteristic patterns of the dual rural economy and dispersed deprivation are manifest. Whilst its scenery is unique, its socio-economic structure would be recognisable within many rural areas. The features of this social exclusion are fully discussed elsewhere in this book. This pattern of a low-wage local economy with a decline in full-time and a growth in part-time employment, persistent gender inequalities, and youth alienation (including drug dependency) is evident for a significant minority. One striking example of the dual economy was the easily-observed fact that most professional jobs were filled by people from outside the area. Locals tended to be concentrated in lower-status occupations.

The Moors does have a reasonably well-developed educational infrastructure. There is a further education college in Scarborough with a campus in Whitby; an outreach centre of Askham Bryan agricultural college in Pickering; a widespread community education service; private and county council-owned training services, delivering Training and Enterprise Council (TEC) contracts; whilst in 2000 the local higher education institution (HEI), University College Scarborough merged with the University of Hull to become its Scarborough Campus. There is a strong voluntary sector which commissions training and education programmes, and the Open University has a healthy recruitment. The Workers' Educational Association (WEA) maintains vibrant local branches and has innovative schemes such as their 'Training on Wheels' programme. In addition, the University of Hull, as the former designated 'Responsible Body', has delivered liberal adult education throughout the region and maintained a small outreach centre in Whitby.

It was in this geographical and educational context that, in 1995, the University of Hull was successful in winning four-year funding from the Higher Education Funding Council for England (HEFCE) for a non-accredited, widening provision project in the North York Moors. In doing so it was consciously addressing its own priorities and commitment to the area. The project was based in what was then the Centre for Continuing Education, Development and Training, now somewhat more snappily titled the Centre for Lifelong Learning. The centre was established with the mainstreaming of continuing education (CE) but was the inheritor of a long tradition of liberal adult education. Its commitment to North Yorkshire had been continuous; but whereas, in Hull, new programmes had been launched in partnership with the voluntary sector for disadvantaged young adults, the Moors had simply maintained its traditional provision. This project sought to augment this programme by new work, specifically addressing rural deprivation and fostering progression into mainstream university provision. Thus the project was aimed both internally, at the centre's reform and restructuring, and externally, at the needs of the rural community.

This case study is primarily descriptive and anecdotal. It does not provide a full account of the work of the project nor does it contain statistical evidence of participation.[1] Some of the data on the socio-economic profile of North Yorkshire is to be found in Chapter Three in this book. Instead, this chapter discusses the development of the project's working relationships and partnerships, seeks to illustrate the process of project development and to raise issues about the nature of CE in rural areas.

The project

Developing a project from scratch is never easy. Hull's first act had been a simple one of plagiarism. The name 'University of the Moors' was a straight lift of the title from the well-established University of the Valleys in South Wales. The project itself was launched with much mis-reporting on the front page of the *Times Higher Education Supplement*. The feature utterly missed the point by reinforcing the rural romanticism that so distorts the debate on rural areas. In a format reproduced in reports of subsequent schemes in the Yorkshire Dales and the Derbyshire Peak District, the article carried a photograph of the member of staff responsible for the project, Daniel Vulliamy, on top of a windswept hill, gazing moodily into the distance. There wasn't even a sheep in sight – let alone a person, a community or a student. The image of rurality that dominates the popular imagination is landscape, not people – and certainly not economic and educational activity.

The HEFCE bid outlined broad aims and objectives, but once the funding was secured these had to be refined. This meant that there had to be an explicit recognition of rural realities and a reappraisal of the university's programme in

North Yorkshire. Four general aims were identified for the project:

- To lay the foundations of a learning society in a remote rural area;
- To address the under-participation of rural communities in lifelong learning;
- To develop partnerships, thereby building an infrastructure to deliver the university's regional role;
- To help rural economic, social and educational development.

The grandiose pretensions of the first aim had more than one eye on current debates in lifelong learning and could be described as purely declaratory. Nonetheless the second and third aims are important elements in any development of a learning society. The explicit focus on rural deprivation meant a reappraisal of the university's work, which in itself required the development of a new infrastructure.

Outreach work established that there were gaps in provision and that participation in adult education showed familiar patterns of overwhelming participation by the more affluent. Their support was critical in ensuring the viability of groups, and thus enabled them to shape curriculum in the area. This was certainly true of the university's provision. Whilst remaining committed to existing students, there was a clear need to expand provision for those groups currently excluded. Low levels of participation in lifelong learning by those sections of rural society implied that there was an untapped market for CE. However, the mere fact that people were not participating meant that the traditional liberal programmes that had previously dominated the university's CE were failing. Innovation was required.

This necessitated the recruitment of new teams of part-time tutors to deliver the programme who were comfortable with widening participation. Their role was not only to deliver curriculum but also to develop it. The quality of the tutors who worked on the project was one of the keys to its successes. This was the new curriculum that was intended to help fulfil the final aim of fostering economic, social and educational development. It had to deliver locally-based progression for local people. It had to be related to their needs both for employment and for further training. Access to professional qualifications would at least enable local people to compete for higher-paid employment.

However, this raised a dilemma. The project funding was for *non-accredited* CE. There is a clear value to this as an entry point to education as it is threat free. Given the decline in the funding for non-accredited work in the wake of the educational utilitarianism of the Conservative government, there was a gap in the market. However, the demand for non-accredited learning was coming predominantly from traditional user groups. Those seeking to develop their careers not only wanted but *needed* accreditation. It was decided to view the funding as supporting non-university accredited work. Open College accreditation was used for the part of the programme, which was designed to promote access to HE. This promptly raised the problems of relationships with other providers. It was clear that partnerships were essential.

The ambition of the general aims was matched by a sense of realism. The project name included 'Towards' in the full knowledge that it was only laying the foundations. Furthermore, rural areas were treated as under-represented *per se*. Therefore the initial emphasis was on developing an infrastructure, rather than targeting specific groups within rural communities. It is hard to see how the project could have progressed otherwise, but the lack of targeting in the early stages was a weakness.

However well-developed local services were, they could not possibly meet the full range of demand and there was a clear need to address the inadequacy of the University of Hull's infrastructure. This resulted in the prioritising of four main developments: partnerships, new centres, dispersed delivery and open learning.

Partnerships

From the outset, the project adopted an explicitly non-competitive approach. In most cases our involvement was welcomed but there were clear concerns about demarcation. It was a policy that the project had to be responsive and sensitive to local needs. The result was the building up of a network of relationships, some of which proved productive whilst some fell away through lack of clear and successful outcomes. It was only through partnerships that the programme prospered. There was an obvious need to effect the maximum reach into rural communities. Hopefully the relationships proved symbiotic rather than parasitic. This was enhanced by the use of Open College accreditation allowing the university to fund pilot programmes that could then be supported (if successful) through other sectors' mainstream funding methodologies.

It also became apparent that the voluntary sector is one of the key partners for any widening provision project. Again, in concentrating on partnerships with educational providers, the potential for targeted provision was grasped too late in the project.

New centres

The first priority was to establish new centres with partners. The university already retained a small outreach centre in Whitby, but the costs of maintaining and staffing such a centre would preclude a similar development elsewhere. Not only that but the centre itself was problematic. It consisted of a suite of excellent, flexible teaching and resource rooms in the Mission to Seamen, a Grade II listed building. Despite the energy and enthusiasm of the tutor organiser, there was a major issue over access. The rooms were on the top floor. Entry at the front meant a lung-bursting climb of three flights of stairs. The back door, used in the evening, was even worse. Entering from a car park, descending steep concrete steps and entering the building via a vertiginous cast iron fire escape, only to meet the stairs half way up, could hardly be seen as disability-friendly. Despite this, the centre was well-used by groups of determined people, and raised the profile of the university in the town. However it proved difficult to extend its use.

The first new centre was established with Askham Bryan College's outreach centre in Pickering, a small market town in a central catchment area for the Ryedale district of North Yorkshire. Here the project funded a new Access programme in the centre, using the premises for open learning tutorials. The Access programme enabled the subsequent development of a part-time degree programme in Social and Behavioural Studies. It enrolled healthily in the early years, picking up on a backlog of latent demand. But numbers fell back after two years, raising questions about long-term viability.

Further premises were used in Scarborough Sixth Form College and in a remarkable centre in the small village of Nawton. 'Opportunities' is the creation of local resident and shop owner, Geoff Gordon. Using a wide range of funding, he converted his shop into a rural resource and training centre. This extraordinary development may have required stamina and patience but is a model of grass-roots independent development, and worthy of a fuller study.

Finally, with the lease due for renewal on the Whitby Centre, it became possible for a move into new voluntary-sector premises with Whitby Network. This is another enterprising development – this time of a redundant cinema, the Coliseum. Although the old centre had done much to establish the university's presence and, despite a number of regrets, the prospect of full disabled access, on site crèche, and integrated provision was too good to miss.

Dispersed provision

If there is one single factor which mitigates against participation in rural areas it is geography. Even the establishment of premises in local centres of population can still fail to reach rural communities. Where travel costs can be prohibitively expensive, or based solely on private transport it can be impossible for people to attend. The cliché about a shrinking world ignores the fact that possibilities for travel are based entirely on wealth. For someone on state benefit, a journey of ten miles could as easily be to the other end of the country. As a result, the project set about the development of a village outreach programme.

The project began taking provision out to smaller communities, using premises such as village halls, libraries, community centres and, occasionally, pubs. This programme was non-accredited and there were some minor successes. These included a local history course for a mixed group of the general public and people with learning difficulties at Botton Village, and an Oral History project in Ruswarp. However, when non-accredited provision was offered elsewhere it did not attract.

The one area where the non-threatening approach of learning without certification was an unqualified success was the Village Information Technology Project. This began as the result of a request by North Yorkshire County Council's community education area officer for North Scarborough. He felt there was a market for computer classes in small locations, something that they could not fund. The tradition of the 'corny' title was maintained and 'Easy PC' was launched. The programme became a huge success. Computer skills are not just vital for employability, they are necessary for social inclusion. Whilst the divide between information-rich and information-poor may be an overdrawn piece of conventional wisdom, computer literacy is as much a life skill as a work skill and there was an insatiable demand in some of the most unlikely places. These ranged from genteel villages to the Foyer residential project for disadvantaged young people in Malton. With students as young as 18 and as old as 80, it was a wonderful lifelong learning experience.

There were three key elements to its success. Firstly, the technology. Twelve laptop computers were bought and established as a peer-to-peer network using radio links. This enabled the use of the latest software in any location and drastically reduced set-up time. The suite could be assembled and dismantled in any setting with an electricity supply in about 15 minutes, and could fit in the boot of a small car. The juxtaposition of old and new – in a remote village hall, where computers were set up on trestle tables with heating provided by a coal fire – was particularly memorable.

One of the disadvantages of the ease of transportation was realised soon after the programme began. The kit was stolen. Anyone can read a leaflet, including thieves. Ironically, this turned out to be the best publicity the programme could have had. It hit the headlines of news-starved local papers and soon the office was getting constant calls asking when the programme would start again. It was now firmly established in the minds of local people. Even so, this rather unorthodox method of publicity is not really to be recommended.

The second element that contributed to the project's success was the structure of the delivery. This consisted of a rolling programme of short courses. Conventional award-bearing programmes are often too long for students to commit themselves to. By running six-week courses at different levels the needs of the local community were met. The visit of 'Easy PC' became one of the local social events in some villages.

Thirdly, any such programme needs good staff. It is easy to see that, given the size of the area, organising the programme would be a logistical nightmare. The project was very lucky in having Stuart Broadhurst as an extraordinarily resourceful, locally-based, part-time tutor. Without him the programme would have foundered at an early stage.

Open learning

It is easy to see open learning as the obvious answer to rural isolation. However, if learning is also isolated, it is hard to see the benefits. Indeed, it can be more difficult to maintain the pressure of learning without the support of a group of fellow learners. Nevertheless (especially given the nature of seasonal and shift work in the rural economy) it is not only a convenient method but, for many, is a safe start without the risk of exposing a fragile self-confidence.

In view of this, good local tutor support proved essential in maintaining progress. The personal relationship between the tutor and the learner was probably the most important factor in successful learning, often developing the materials through additional resources. Where possible, meetings were arranged in our outreach centres, but for some students with disabilities meetings were arranged in the home. In those cases, the tutor's ability to absorb overwhelming hospitality was tested to the full.

The Moors programme was 'low-tech'. It relied on paper-based, Open University Access material with Open College Network accreditation. The small cohorts of students did well and were able, in some instances, to meet as small groups. However, given the development of new technology, there are considerable possibilities. The university's Internet learning platform, Merlin, offers potential for electronic delivery of new programmes.

Once the infrastructure had been established, it was then possible to extend partnership activities to specifically-targeted excluded groups. The problem hinged on the limitations of four-year funding. The initial year was spent in development, the second and third year in building the infrastructure, and it was only in the final year that specifically targeted work could be established. The full period of the funding had merely taken the project to the starting post.

Two examples of initiatives are worth discussing. The first scheme was the Alternative Learning Project for disadvantaged young adults. This emerged from a partnership with community education and Ryedale Detached Youth Service. The target group was disaffected young adults, and the aim was to reintegrate them into learning. The project was successful in winning funding from the Further Education Funding Council via community education, and employed two part-time development workers. The university funded some small-scale provision but there was room for further developments.

Secondly, planning took place with the Whitby Disabled Action Group as a result of a member's involvement with our open learning scheme. The learner herself was dynamic in forcing collaboration and was justly proud of her achievement. The project is now being taken forward by Whitby Network as part of the Coliseum development.

In both these cases the university was not the leading player but one of the catalysts for development. The question of its role as a HE institution was never resolved. Pre-degree provision could always be questioned by other sectors worried about competition for students. Given the nature of numbers-driven funding formulae, this is inevitable. Prior to mainstreaming, university CE had an accepted niche position within adult education. Now it seeks to be the locus of widening participation and part-time accredited learning. Arguably, this is a revitalisation of its original aims. However, there appears to be a reluctance of policy makers to recognise this tradition of second-chance learning through universities.[2] The recognition of HE as something other than a receiver of qualified students and, instead, an active participant in outreach and widening participation has still to be won.

'bundles', which together tell a logical story. For example, 'access to services' would be measured by combining indicators on areas with no shop (or some other service), areas with no regular bus service and households with no car. This would account for all those with no local shop and no transport to shops elsewhere. Another proposed 'bundle' covers 'access to employment opportunities'. It would measure the registered unemployed, the 'hidden unemployed' and working-age people who recently moved out of the area (probably to look for work). An advantage of the 'bundles' approach is that it counts the actual number of people exposed to a particular aspect of disadvantage.

Eight 'bundles' of indicators are proposed, relating to different aspects of rural disadvantage. These are: access to employment; quality of employment; vulnerability of employment; housing affordability; housing quality; low incomes; access to services; and isolation. It may be that different 'bundles' would be relevant to different policy applications.[4]

This approach would be one way in which the necessary developments could be funded if money is to be committed to rural widening participation. However, whilst this may contribute to reducing social exclusion by helping establish a process of social mobility amongst some sections of rural society, it is hard to see it being successful in reversing the trend towards polarisation. This is graphically described by Derek Brown as a process which is producing 'a rapidly-growing social gap, as serious as the so-called north-south divide or the national gap between rich and poor. That is, the gulf of incomes and opportunities between the rural affluent and the rural deprived.' He continues:

> The polarisation is accelerating as wealthy people move to parts of the countryside where farm incomes are falling, and unemployment remains stubbornly high. In the Cotswolds, the quintessence of the rural idyll and the full- or part-time home of many rich newcomers, 27 per cent of households have annual incomes of less than £7,000. In a Wiltshire village surveyed by the Countryside Agency, a third of households had incomes below £6,000, while another third had more than £40,000 ...

> As many as one in six of young adults born in rural communities are leaving for the cities because they can no longer afford to live in the country. And those who stay face a grim task finding work. Unemployment figures for rural areas are often grotesquely distorted: by the influx of retired newcomers, the inclusion of country-dwellers who commute to work in towns, and by the relatively large proportion of part-time and seasonal jobs. More telling than any number of raw statistics, however, are the comments from case studies. One farming couple in the Peak District, somehow living on a quarter of the national minimum wage, comment: 'When we got this farm it was a dream come true. But it's a nightmare now.' A farm worker who has been without work for nine years tells how 'the bottom dropped out of our world.' And an 18-year-old Cornish youth, both jobless and homeless, poignantly records: 'Life was great until I hit 12.'[5]

It is only realistic to underline that whilst projects like 'Towards a University of the Moors' can have an enormous impact on individuals' lives, they can not provide a solution to the gulf between rich and poor. To do this means the embracing of an egalitarian political economy that seems to be rejected by New Labour and is certainly anathema to the Countryside Alliance. Much now depends on the Regional Development Agencies, but it is hard to be optimistic.

Notes

1. Further details are available from the author at the Centre for Lifelong Learning.
2. One example is the decision to exclude HE from eligibility for the use of Individual Learning Accounts within the new national framework.
3. Lukes, S. (1974). *Power: A Radical View*. Macmillan.
4. The Countryside Commission (1998). *Rural Disadvantage – Understanding the Processes*. Research Note, RDR 36/S.
5. *The Guardian*, June 15 2000.

Index

Note: the words 'tables', 'maps', or 'figures' following page numbers refer to tables, maps or figures in the text, e.g. 96(table)